JESUIT LATIN POETS

JESUIT LATIN POETS
OF THE 17TH AND 18TH CENTURIES
AN ANTHOLOGY OF NEO-LATIN POETRY

SELECTED AND PARAPHRASED BY
JAMES J. MERTZ, S.J.

EDITED AND ANNOTATED BY
JOHN P. MURPHY, S.J.

IN COLLABORATION WITH
JOZEF IJSEWIJN

BOLCHAZY-CARDUCCI PUBLISHERS

This Publication was made possible by
PEGASUS LIMITED

Design by
BERNARD BURKE

©Copyright 1989
BOLCHAZY-CARDUCCI PUBLISHERS
1000 Brown Street
Wauconda, Illinois 60084

Printed in the United States of America

International Standard Book Number:
Hardbound   0-86516-214-X
Softbound   0-86516-215-8

Library of Congress Catalog Number:
88-62698

Library of Congress Cataloging-in-Publication Data

Mertz, James J.
   Jesuit Latin poets of the 17th and 18th centuries : an anthology
of neo-Latin poetry / selected and paraphrased by James J. Mertz,
S.J. ; edited and annotated by John P. Murphy, S.J. in collaboration
with Jozef IJsewijn.
     p.   cm.
   English and Latin.
   Bibliography: p.
   ISBN 0-86516-214-X : $39.00. — ISBN 0-86516-215-8 (pbk.) : $24.00
   1. Jesuit poetry, Latin (Medieval and modern)   2. Jesuit poetry
Latin (Medieval and modern)—Translations into English.   3. English
poetry—Translations from Latin.   I. Murphy, John P.   II. IJsewijn,
Jozef.   III. Title.
PA8133.J46M47   1989
871'.04080922—dc20   88-62698
                                                                                                                    CIP

INTRODUCTION

This anthology of neo-Latin poetry is the fruit of many years of teaching and study on the part of James J. Mertz, S.J. Fr. Mertz, Loyola's "Mister Chips," tried very hard to finish his book on the Jesuit Latin poets, but ill health and the frailties of his nineties made that impossible. I had helped Fr. Mertz with the project and was somewhat familiar with the matter and with Father's plans. It was, however, not until the academic year of 1986-87 that I was able to devote to the Jesuit Latin poets the effort needed for completion of the book. The time, the research materials, and equipment were supplied by Loyola University of Chicago through an academic leave. I am very grateful for the opportunity to complete the book, and, in Fr. Mertz's name and my own, I thank all at Loyola of Chicago who made this work possible. Further on I will make explicit mention of individuals who contributed to the project, but I should like to begin with a sketch of Fr. James J. Mertz's long and fruitful life.

James J. Mertz, S.J. was born on May 24, 1882 at Toledo, Ohio. He was the firstborn of nine children to August and Catherine Homer Mertz. His early education was at St. Peter and Paul's school in Toledo and Canisius High School in Buffalo, New York.

On August 31, 1900 he entered the Buffalo Mission of the Society of Jesus at what was then called South Brooklyn, Ohio, and today is Parma. He had his novitiate and juniorate (humanistic studies) at St. Stanislaus in South Brooklyn from 1900 to 1904. He then went to Prairie du Chien, Wisconsin, for philosophical studies at Sacred Heart College. He did two of the customary three years of philosophy at Prairie du Chien and was awarded his A.B. by that institution in 1905. There followed five years of regency (high school teaching) at St. John's, Toledo from 1906 to 1911. In addition to the expected subjects of Latin and German, Fr. Mertz also taught geography and natural science. In this versatility, Fr. Mertz resembles the Jesuit Latin poets whose works he collected and translated/paraphrased.

Upon the completion of regency, Fr. Mertz went to St. Louis to complete his third year of philosophy (1911-12), then the four years of theology (1912-16). As had been the custom in the Society of Jesus, Fr. Mertz was ordained to the priesthood at the end of his third year of theology. That occurred on June 30, 1915 and the ordaining bishop was John Cardinal Glennon. In 1917, St. Louis University conferred upon Fr. Mertz a Master of Arts degree. The diploma has the unusual stipulation that it is retroactive, for it states that the rank and privileges date from 1912. Father's master's thesis was *Horace and the Modern Poets*.

During 1916-17, Fr. Mertz taught at St. John's College in Toledo. The following year, 1917-18, was devoted to the tertianship or third year of novitiate, once again at St. Stanislaus in what was now called Brooklyn Station (Parma), Ohio. For 1918-19, Fr. Mertz taught at Campion College in Prairie du Chien. There he pronounced his final vows in the Society of Jesus as a Spiritual Coadjutor on March 25, 1919. Almost 50 years later, Father was given the solemn profession (February 2, 1968). At Campion College, Father added philosophy and English to his repertoire of teaching subjects.

From 1919 to 1922, Fr. Mertz taught at St. Ignatius High School in Chicago, Illinois. In 1922, Fr. Mertz was a member of the small band of Jesuits who travelled to the north side of Chicago to begin college level classes at the Lake Shore Campus of Loyola of Chicago. For fifty years until his retirement on August 4, 1972, Fr. Mertz was identified with the classics department and Loyola. In the classroom, Father taught many classical authors, but his specialty was later Latin. He took students through patristic authors, medieval Latin (the last course he taught was in this), and the post-Renaissance Jesuit Latin poets. He also excelled as a preacher and was much in demand in the 20's and 30's. For example, he preached to a congregation of over 100,000 at the Eucharistic Congress in Soldier Field in 1926. Fr. Mertz was also a builder and almost single-handedly raised the funds and oversaw the construction of Madonna della Strada chapel on the Lake Shore Campus. Father dedicated much time and effort from 1924 to 1937 to this building project. Madonna della Strada was dedicated in 1938 and was in constant use thereafter though construction work continued. Finally, Fr. Mertz was also an administrator. He was chairman of the classics department at Loyola University of Chicago from 1931 to 1960. He served as President of the Chicago Classical Club from 1940 to 1942. It was to this group that Father gave lectures on the Jesuit Latin poets Sarbiewski and Balde. Eventually the talks were redone for articles in *Classical Bulletin*. He also served as President for the Illinois Classical Conference from 1941 to 1943. He organized the Jesuit Family Club in Chicago and founded the Pi Sigma Alpha fraternity to help in raising funds for the chapel.

Fr. Mertz did not allow retirement from the classroom and two major illnesses to end his work. For he produced a small book on the building of Madonna della Strada chapel and was at work on the Jesuit Latin poets when the end came on January 29, 1979 in Father's ninety-seventh year of life. In the Introduction he was preparing for the volume, Father Mertz wrote, "I publish this volume as a permanent record of one phase of my half-century of academic service to Loyola University." I have the distinct pleasure of completing Father's work and preparing it for publication.

On the subject of Latin literature, Fr. Mertz was definitely of the opinion that there was a continuity from ancient times to the modern era. He felt it particularly appropriate that he, as a Jesuit priest, teach Christian Latin. A study of Loyola's course schedules from over the years reveals that Fr. Mertz frequently taught courses in the Latin Fathers, Prudentius, and Medieval Latin. Later, Father became interested in the Jesuit Latin poets. This was partly due to the prodding of Fr. William T. Kane, S.J., who was Loyola's librarian and who took great pains to build up the University's *Jesuitica* collection. The Jesuit Fathers at St. Ignatius High School in Chicago also merit high praise for giving the collection a solid base. Without any doubt, Loyola's collection of Jesuit Latin poets surpasses any other American library's. It is mainly the result of Father Kane's efforts that detailed research in the Jesuit Latin poets is possible in Loyola University's special collections.

As stated above, Fr. Mertz came to the Jesuit Latin poets relatively late in his academic life. As far as a formal course is concerned, he first taught the Jesuit Latin poets in the summer of 1940. Other times that he taught them were: I Sem. 1944, II Sem. 1947, I Sem.

1962, Summer 1965, and II Sem. 1968. The selection of poems and their translations/paraphrases stem from the texts of poems that Father prepared for these courses.

The poems in this anthology were selected and paraphrased by Fr. Mertz. The changes in the text and translations/paraphrases introduced by the editor are so minimal that they will not be noted. Most changes in the Latin were due to a preference for classical spellings rather than Renaissance ones. Although Fr. Mertz and some others such as Miss Donna Majeske and Mrs. Kathryn Krug have worked on the biographies of the Jesuit poets, the biographical sketches that appear in this volume are mostly the editor's work. Father left almost no annotations and so these, too, are to be ascribed to the editor. Professor Jozef IJsewijn of the Catholic University of Louvain has kindly assisted with forms and spellings of names and with many other technical matters. Finally, Father Mertz was accustomed to refer to his field of interest as the "Jesuit Latin poets of the 16th and 17th Centuries." Although there are some Jesuit poets whose works were written in the 16th century, none is in the present anthology. Some few, however, are in the 18th century. So the editor has judged it best to entitle the book *The Jesuit Latin Poets of the 17th and 18th Centuries*.

The Jesuit Latin poets certainly subscribed to the Horatian view expressed in the *Ars Poetica* that literature should mingle the pleasurable with the profitable. They wished that their students not only appreciate beautiful literature, but also that they would be uplifted and edified at the same time. Latin was still the *lingua franca* of Europe and an educated person was expected to be able to write Latin, even in complicated verse forms. Furthermore, the Jesuits, especially in the Hapsburg realms, hoped that there would be a return to a Europe unified in faith and language. The Jesuits believed in the value of imitation in writing and the modeling of one's style on the classics. There were things, however, in the classics that they found unacceptable and therefore avoided. Examples of this would be praise of Venus, love for female paramours, and still more, love of little boys. In the place of physical loves, we find the blessed Virgin and the saints, though the Jesuit poets use many of the same words and expressions for them. (*Divus*, for example, now means

"Saint" or "holy" rather than "deified" or "divine.") Neo-Stoic ideas are also acceptable to the Jesuit Latin poets. So we find themes such as the fickleness of fortune, shortness of life, the sufficiency of virtue, and fortitude in adversity. The praise of nature is also a subject common to the classics and the Jesuit Latin poets. Our collection contains poems on birds, the cicada, and the seasons. The convention of addressing the lyre also does nothing to compromise faith; so we read two poems on that theme in this anthology.

The field of Jesuit Latin poetry is vast. Fr. Mertz limited his study to some 40 poets whose editions were readily available to him in the Loyola University library. He noted, however, that in the Southern Netherlands alone there were some 225 Jesuit Latin poets before the suppression of the Society of Jesus in 1773. Also that province (*p. flandro-belgica*) produced a magnificent emblem book in 1640 with the title *Imago Primi Saeculi* (*Image of the First Century*). The work extols the Society of Jesus on the occasion of the first century of its existence. Many members of the province contributed poems anonymously to this volume. It is estimated that there were 500 colleges at the time of the Society's suppression in 1773, at every one of which there was a professor of Latin. Many of these zealous teachers produced "wholesome" poetry for their young charges. For the present anthology, Fr. Mertz selected poems from nineteen Jesuit Latin poets. Sarbiewski and Balde contribute far and away the most poems, but that is understandable since they are the most important Jesuit Latin poets and constituted the core of the course Father Mertz taught in the matter. However, the Jesuit poets of England (Edmund Campion and Robert Southwell, for example) and the Americas, Diego Abad and Rafael Landivar, for example) are omitted in this anthology.

I would like to end this brief introduction with a sincere word of thanks to Bro. Michael J. Grace, S.J., Loyola University of Chicago's archivist and Ms. Valerie Browne, the assistant archivist. I spent many hours with them in the university archives, consulting the 17th and 18th century texts and the files on Fr. Mertz's work on the Jesuit Latin poets. Because of this fine collection, I was able to consult earlier versions of Mertz's translations of the poems. The critical apparatus after the translations in the anthology lists variant readings from this source in the archives and indicate alternate versions that Fr. Mertz considered. The Latin variants are so rare that I have restricted mention of them to the notes. The list of books that follows represents only the sources for the texts in the anthology. Thanks to Loyola's excellent collection and Bro. Grace's kind help, I was able to consult many more "primary sources," thus achieving a fuller picture of the scope of each poet's work.

John P. Murphy, S.J.
Loyola University of Chicago

TABLE OF CONTENTS

Introduction	v-x
Table of Contents	xi-xiv
List of Illustrations	xv-xvi
Sources of Latin in the Anthology	xvii

Matthias Casimir Sarbiewski   1-51

Life		1-3
Poem 1:	Youth isn't everything	4-5
Poem 2:	Fickle is fate in all things human	6-9
Poem 3:	Life's brief span is stretched by goodness	10-11
Poem 4:	To His Lyre	12-13
Poem 5:	At leisure, the author declares war on the vices of his day	14-15
Poem 6:	To Narvia	16-19
Poem 7:	From the Song of Songs of Solomon	20-23
Poem 8:	Vain are the tombs and monuments of kings	24-27
Poem 9:	Keep the even tenor of your way even in adversity	28-29
Poem 10:	To the Barberini Bees: Coming of the Honeyed Age	30-31
Poem 11:	Why he sang so joyfully on his way	32-33
Poem 12:	To the Rose	34-35
Poem 13:	To Jesus the Greatest Good	36-37
Poem 14:	To the Cicada	38-39
Poem 15:	To the Fountain, Sona	40-41
Poem 16:	To the Boy Jesus	42-43
Poem 17:	To the Dew	44-47
Poem 18:	Epigrams	48-51

Johannes Kreihing   52-61

Life		52-53
Poem 19:	England Today	54-55
Poem 20:	Winter comes and the human body freezes	56-57

Poem 21: His fever and his doctor	58-59
Poem 22: St. Monica to her son, St. Augustine	60-61
Bernard Van Bauhuysen	62-67
Life	62-63
Poem 23: What brings peace and friends	64-65
Poem 24: Who's a friend?	66-67
Nicolas Avancini	68-75
Life:	68-69
Poem 25: In Sickness	70-71
Poem 26: To know oneself is supreme science	72-75
Charles Malapert	76-83
Life	76-77
Poem 27: Against Lucas Osiander	78-81
Poem 28: The Pettifogger	82-83
Sidronius De Hossche	84-91
Life	84-87
Poem 29: To Sleep	88-91
Jacob Vande Walle	92-95
Life	92-93
Poem 30: To Sidronius De Hossche	94-95
Jacob Balde	96-147
Life	96-99
Poem 31: The Constancy of Thomas More	100-103
Poem 32: In Praise of Wine	104-105
Poem 33: The Stein of Beer	106-107
Poem 34: To Thinness	108-111
Poem 35: A Dirge for the Funeral of a Rich Man	112-115
Poem 36: A box tree trimmed in the figure of a boy in the formal gardens of Albert	116-119
Poem 37: The Dance of Death	120-123
Poem 38: To Sleep	124-129
Poem 39: To Mary on the Vigil of her Assumption	130-131
Poem 40: His Finch	132-135
Poem 41: The Heliotrope	136-139

Poem 42: To the Blessed Virgin for a Happy Death	140-143
Poem 43: The author despises all funeral pomp and ceremony	144-147

René Rapin — 148-151
Life — 148-149
Poem 44: To a Cicada — 150-151

Jacob Masen — 152-163
Life — 152-155
Poem 45: A stupid old man who still longs for money — 156-159
Poem 46: Pride lowers the dignity of man — 160-163

Charles de la Rue — 164-167
Life — 164-165
Poem 47: For the Nobility of France — 166-167

Noel Étienne Sanadon — 168-173
Life — 168-169
Poem 48: On the Death of a Canary — 170-171
Poem 49: Cupid Stung by a Bee — 172-173

Daniel Ramus — 174-179
Life — 174-175
Poem 50: Death of a Parrot — 176-179

François J. T. Desbillons — 180-183
Life — 180-181
Poem 51: The New Orpheus — 182-183

Tarquinio Galluzzi — 184-191
Life — 184-185
Poem 52: On Torquato Tasso's Grave — 186-187
Poem 53: The Ruins of Ancient Rome — 188-189
Poem 54: To the New Rome — 190-191

Vincenzo Guiniggi — 192-201
Life — 192-193
Poem 55: The Tightrope Walker — 194-197

Poem 56: A Cicada Singing to the Lyre	198-199
Poem 57: The Tomb of the Dying Year	200-201
Giannantonio Bernardi	202-205
Life	202-203
Poem 58: The Old Man - a Fop	204-205
Giacomo Lubrani	206-211
Life	206-207
Poem 59: Philip Neri	208-209
Poem 60: Iced drinks in the summertime	210-211
Lieven De Meyere	212-221
Life	212-213
Poem 61: Praise of Horace, Prince of Poets	214-217
Poem 62: The Agony and Hopelessness of Gout	218-221
Index of *Incipits*	223-225
Index of Names and Themes	227-229

ILLUSTRATIONS

1. The portrait of Sarbiewski is taken from Alfred Hamy: *Galerie illustreê de la Compagnie de Jesu.* 9 vols. Paris, 1893. This and all other illustrations come from the *Jesuitica* collection of Loyola University of Chicago's Cudahy Library. Patti Schor of the University's Center for Instructional Design kindly and expertly provided the photographs.   1

2. From the *Imago Primi Saeculi Societatis Jesu a provincia flandro-belgica eiusdem Societatis representata.* Antwerp, 1640.   52

3. From the 1634 Antwerp edition of the *Epigrammata.* The Latin form of the poet's name is *Bauhusius;* the French *Bauhuis.*   62

4. From the 1674-75 Cologne edition of Avancini's *Poesis dramatica.* 5 vols. in 3.   68

5. Portrait of Francis Coster from Hamy.   76

6. Portrait of Sidronius De Hossche from Hamy.   84

7. From *Sidronii Hoschii e Societate Iesu Elegiarum Libri VI.* Nuremberg, 1755.   92

8. Portrait of Jacob Balde from Hamy   96

9. Portrait of René Rapin from Hamy   148

10. Title page of Masen's *Epitome Annalium Trevirensium.* Trier, 1676.   152

11. Portrait of Charles de la Rue from Hamy.   164

12. Portrait of Noel Sanadon from Hamy.   169

13. Title page of Frederic Reiffenberg's *Patrum S.J. ad Rhenum inferiorem poemata.* Cologne, 1758.   174

14. Portrait of F.J.T. Desbillons from Hamy.   180

15. Title page of Tarquinio Galluzzi's *Carminum Libri III.* Rome, 1630.   184

16. Illustration from Vincenzo Guiniggi's *Poesis heroica, elegiaca, lyrica, epigrammatica...item dramatica.* Antwerp, 1637.   192

17. From the *Imago Primi Saeculi*. 202

18. Illustration from Giacomo Lubrani's *Suaviludia Musarum ad Sebethi ripam Epigrammaton Libri X*. Naples, 1690. 206

19. Title page and illustration from Lievin De Meyere's *Poematum Libri VI*. Brussels, 1703. 212

SOURCES OF LATIN TEXTS IN THIS ANTHOLOGY

Avancini, Nicolas: POESIS LYRICA. Vienna, 1659.

Balde, Jacob: CARMINA LYRICA. Munich, 1844.

Bernardi, Giannantonio: CARMINA. Bologna, 1765.

De Hossche, Sidronius: S. HOSSCHII S.J. ELEGIARUM LIBRI VI. Antwerp, 1656.

de la Rue, Charles: CARMINUM LIBRI IV. Antwerp, 1693.

De Meyere, Lieven: POEMATUM LIBRI VI. Brussels, 1703.

Desbillons, François Joseph: FABULARUM AESOPIARUM LIBRI V. Paris, 1759.

Galluzzi, Tarquinio: CARMINUM LIBRI III. Rome, 1611.

Guiniggi, Vincenzo: POESIS HEROICA, ELEGIACA, LYRICA, EPIGRAMMATICA...ITEM DRAMATICA. Rome, 1627

Kreihing, Johannes: POEMATA APOSCHOLOMASTICA. Frankfurt, 1658.

Lubrani, Giacomo: SUAVILUDIA MUSARUM AD SEBETHI RIPAM. EPIGRAMMATUM LIBRI X. Naples, 1690.

Malapert, Charles: POEMATA. Antwerp, 1616.

Masen, Jacob: selections are taken from Frederic Reiffenberg's PATRUM S.J. AD RHENUM INFERIOREM POEMATA. Köln, 1758.

Ramus, Daniel: selections are taken from Frederic Reiffenberg's PATRUM S.J. AD RHENUM INFERIOREM POEMATA. Köln, 1758.

Rapin, René: CARMINA MULTO QUAM ANTEA EMENDATIORA. Venice, 1733.

Sanadon, Noel Étienne: CARMINUM LIBRI QUATTUOR. Paris, 1715.

Sarbiewski, Matthias Casimir: POEMATA OMNIA. Stara Wies, 1892.

Van Bauhuysen, Bernard: EPIGRAMMATUM SELECTORUM LIBRI V. Antwerp, 1616.

Vande Walle, Jacob: IACOBI WALLII E SOCIETATE IESU POEMATUM LIBRI IX. Antwerp, 1656.

Matthias Casimir Sarbiewski
(1595-1640)

The Horace of Poland

Matthias Casimir Sarbiewski (Sarbievius), the Horace of Poland, was born near Plonsk in the Duchy of Masovia on February 24, 1595. He entered the Society of Jesus at Vilna on July 25, 1612. After teaching grammar, the humanities, and rhetoric in the College of Nobles at Kroze and at Polotsk, he took up his theological studies at Vilna in 1620 and finished the course in Rome where he was ordained in 1623.

Maffeo Cardinal Barberini, elected Pope Urban VIII on August 26, 1623 and a poet in his own right, patronized the young Jesuit, who hailed the pope with an ode to the bees emblazoned on the Barberini crest (*Odes* 3.15; number 10 in this collection). Urban crowned Sarbiewski *Poeta Laureatus* in the capital. During his stay in Rome, Sarbiewski worked on the revision of the breviary hymns with Famiano Strada, S.J. (1572-1649), Tarquinio Galluzzi, S.J. (1574-1649), and Girolamo Petrucci, S.J. (1585-1669) under Pope Urban VIII. Sarbiewski returned to Poland to spend the rest of his life in teaching, preaching, and acting as chaplain to King Ladislaus IV (reigned 1632-1648). Sarbiewski died in Warsaw on April 2, 1640. He was buried without any grave markings in the Jesuit church.

In the course of time, due to the suppression of the Society of Jesus in 1773, his remains and those of other Jesuits came into the charitable care of the Fathers of the Pious Schools. During a renovation of their church, the graves were found but only a few letters of an inscription could be deciphered. Those that were legible are: *Po...Laur. S...* The conjecture is that these identified Sarbiewski's coffin: *Po(eta) Laur(eatus) S(arbievius)*. Later he was buried in the cemetery Pawazkowska, and in 1888 the following inscription was placed on a monument dedicated to him:

Mathiae Casimiro Sarbiewski, nato Sarbieviae in Masovia, die 24 Febr. 1595, vita functo Varsaviae die 2 April, 1640, Ladislai IV regis oratori a sacris poetae inclyto laurea Urbani VIII P.M. manu coronato, quod arte Horatio par, mente excelsior, fidem resque moresque maiorum carminibus latinis perpulchris extollendo, gentis suae nomen mire apud exteros auxerit, posteri memores.

To Matthias Casimir Sarbiewski born at Castle Sarbievo in Masovia on February 24, 1595, and deceased at Warsaw on April 2, 1640. He was court preacher for King Ladislaus IV. Urban VIII, the Supreme Pontiff, crowned him with laurel as an outstanding poet because he was the equal to Horace in art and loftier than he in thought. He extolled the faith, the deeds, and the character of his ancestors with very beautiful Latin poems. He marvelously increased the renown of his people with outsiders. Mindful of all this, we, members of a later generation, (have erected this monument).

It is strange that the letters "S.J." or "S.I." do not appear on the plaque. Sarbiewski's fame is as wide as the world of letters. Gifted with remarkable talents in music and the fine arts, Sarbiewski shows forth as a poet of lofty and sustained flights of imagination, rivaling Horace, whose poems he knew by heart, and Pindar, whose odes he imitated. His lyrics show his mind and heart. They are concerned with themes of love and devotion to Christ Crucified, to our Blessed Lady, to his many friends, especially his lifelong friend Stanislaus Lubienski, the Bishop of Plock, and Francesco Cardinal Barberini, the nephew of Pope Urban VIII, whom he lauds as his Maecenas in several of his poems of exquisite finish. Some of his noblest efforts are found in his patriotic poems addressed primarily to the Polish nobility. The nobles are urged to cease hostilities toward their fellow Europeans and Christians, and to direct their bellicose spirits against the Turks. Sarbiewski's tenderest pieces, in which he rivals the grace of Horace himself, are those in praise of the rose, the violet, and the cicada. In recognition of his accomplishments King Ladislaus IV also crowned him poet laureate.

As a religious Sarbiewski was known for his love of solitude, turning from the court to prayer and study. He found the chaplaincy to the king very trying. He had the physical strength to take part in the hunt, but on one occasion did not do so. Embarrassed as he was by his failure to participate, he remained in the hunters' lodge where he claimed he composed some odes on nature in imitation of Pindar. These have been called *Silviludia (Pleasant Diversions)* in the printed editions, but see the note to our selection from the *Silviludia (number 17)* for a brief discussion of the current critical position on the authenticity of those poems. The selection given in this anthology is entitled, "The Dew of Morn."

Sarbiewski's poems have been translated into Polish, French, German, Italian, English, Dutch, and Czech. His poems in honor of the Blessed Virgin have especially appealed to translators.

Poem 1

Liber I, Ode IV
Ad Crispum Laevinium
Ne nimiun adulescentiae fidat

Vive iucundae metuens iuventae,
Crispe Laevini: fugiunt avarae
Mensium lunae, nimiumque volvi
    Lubricus aether.

5   Tu licet multo pretiosus auro,
Gemmea vestem moderere zona,
Et super collo Tyrias amicet
    Fibula lanas:

Iure Phoenissis vaga penna cristis
10   Stare labenti dubitat galero:
Iure, quo fulges, timidum refigi
    Palluit aurum.

Quod tibi larga dedit hora dextra,
Hora furaci rapiet sinistra,
15   More fallentis tenerum iocose
    Matris alumnum.

Mobiles rerum dubiique casus
Regna mortalis tenuere vitae:
Sedulus metae, properat fugacis
20   Impetus aevi.

Tardius ponto volat Adriano,
Quam ratem mersi pepulere remi,
Et repentinis animosa trudunt
    Carbasa ventis.

25   Omnibus mundi Dominator horis
Aptat urgendas per inane pennas:
Pars adhuc nido latet, et futuros
    Crescit in annos.

---

1. *live...life*: go on living;   1. *yeasty youth*: Keep your youth in mind; Respect your youth; Youth isn't everything;   2. *speed by*: speeding...fast;   3. *changeable*: changes so often (frequent);   4. *it's*: tis, though;   6: *arrange*: gather; straighten;   8. *coat*: mantle;   22. *boat*: barge;   27. *and will*: only to.

Meter: Sapphic strophe

Title: This Laevinius (Lewinski?) may be the companion of Sarbiewski on his return from Rome in 1625 (thus Wall in the 1892 edition). But even if Sarbiewski had specific individuals in mind, it is most likely that he gave them fictional Roman names.

Poem 1

Book 1, Ode 4
To Crispus Laevinius
Youth isn't everything

Live your own life. Be wary of yeasty youth,
My dear Crispus. The monthly moons speed by and
The weather is so uncertain and changeable. (5)

It's true you are wealthy,
And arrange your clothes with a jeweled belt
And your imported woolen coat is fastened at the neck with a brooch,

While a feather with a purple crest
Sways fluttering in your flanging tam-o'shanter.

Remember! What a happy hour gave you so generously
A darker one will snatch away...
Like a mother at play with her infant son. (15)

Many changes and doubtful moods
Determine the rule of mortal life;
There's always in the fleeting years the push to get on. (20)

The boat in the Adriatic moves more slowly
Than the one propelled by oars
Or the billowing sails of a sudden gust of wind.

The Lord of all at all hours adapts us to meet the unknown. (25)
Some things are still hidden in the nest
And will grow to meet the future.

Text:

1. "Yeasty youth" is Mertz's attempt to capture the alliteration of *iucundae iuventae*.

2. *avarae lunae*: greedy, impatient moons; the epithet is transferred to an impersonal thing as at Virgil *Aen.* 3.44 *"litus avarum,"* the shore line covered with wreckage.

4. *lubricus aether*: quick changing; contrast with Horace's *"nimium lubricus vultus"* (*Carm.* I.19.8), which means "seductive."

7. *amicet*: From *amicare*, "to make friends." Sarbiewski refers to a brooch that pins the clothes together.

9. *Phoenissis cristis*: refers to Phoenicia in Syria; metonymy for purple.

10. *labenti galero*: the *galerum* (also *galerus*) was a cap of fur, a skull cap, a wig (Juvenal); here it is probably a tam-o'shanter, the style of hat worn at that time. Mertz translated *labenti* with "flanging". He failed to give a version of verses 11 and 12.

15. *More fallentis matris*: a picture of a mother playing with her child, her right hand giving, her left hand taking away.

24. *carbasa*: Spanish flax, linen, sails, as in English "canvas". The point of the comparison is that our life situation changes more swiftly than a ship is tossed in heavy weather.

27. *pars adhuc nido latet*: The words have become a proverb: "The future is concealed from us."

Poem 2

Liber I, Ode VII
Ad Telephum Lycum

Fortunae rerumque humanarum inconstantiam accusat

    Eheu, Telephe, ludimur:
        Fortunae volucri ludimur impetu!
    Aeternum nihil est, sacro
        Quidquid lenta tulit materies sinu.
5   Statur casibus. Occidet
        Quod surgit: sed adhuc surget, et occidet
    Ritu praecipitis pilae,
        Quae cum pulsa cava reicitur manu,
    Nunc leves secat Africos,
10   Nunc terrae refugis absilit ictibus.
    Vesper vespere truditur:
        Sed nunc deterior, nunc melior subit.
    Anni nubibus insident,
        Incertis equitant lustra Favoniis,
15   Caeco saecula turbine.
        Haec, quam Pieria decipimus lyra,
    Iuncto fulminis essedo,
        Eheu! quam celeres hora quatit Notos!
    Nec gratae strepitum lyrae,
20   Nec curat miserae carmina tibiae:
    Et quamquam canitur levis,
        Sese tota suis laudibus invidet.
    Magnas interea rapit
        Urbesque et populos, et miserabili
25   Reges subruit impetu;
        Et sceptri decus, et regna cadentium
    Permiscet cineri ducum,
        Auratasque trabes, et penetralia,
    Et cives simul et super

---

5. *flow:* flux;   7. *with cupped hand:* with the hand;   8. Adds: and then;   8. *changed:* quick;   13. *in unknown whirl:* in darkening storms;   14. *sweet:* soft;   15. *daylight's:* lightning's;   18. *blast:* blare;   21. *As life is lived:* the while we live;   22. *crowds:* peoples, cities;   24. *grave:* dust;   27. *lordly mounds:* lofty heap.

Meter: Second Asclepiadean system.

Poem 2

Book 1, Ode 7
To Telephus Lycus

Fickle is fate in all things human

    Alas, dear Telephus, we are all deceived
        By playful Fortune in her giddy whirl.
    There's nothing in the sacred lap of time
        That ever lasts beyond the fleeting years.
5   In constant flow things grow and then decline,
        And still will change with each succeeding turn.
    Like tennis ball that's batted with cupped hand
        Will quickly bounce to earth with changed retards.
    The hours of night are by night's hours replaced,
10   And one night's darker and the other's bright.
    The days are oft o'ercast by darker clouds,
        And years ride on like clouds in western skies
    As centuries are replaced in unknown whirl.
    The while we sing the Muses' sweet refrain,
15   We ride along in daylight's speedy car.
        Alas, how fast the hours boom forth their change!
    We fail to hear the graceful lyric note,
        Or e'en the fanfare of the trumpet's blast;
    And though we sing a song of sweet refrain,
20   Dame Fortune envies each who steals her praise.
    As life is lived she whelms in bitter doom
        Great cities with their crowds and the pride of
    Kings that rule in royal diadem.
        She mingles in the grave both great and small,
25   The golden palace and the poor man's hut,
        And all the pride lies hidden in the dust.
    Above the lordly mounds of worldly pomp,
        And funeral pyres of the mightiest men,
    She speeds along as queen, in triumph bold.

Title: Cf *Romeo and Juliet* III.5.60: "O, fortune, fortune! all men call thee fickle." Telephus Lycus seems to be fictional. The name appears three times in Horace's *Carmina*: 3.19.26; 1.13.1; 4.11.21. None of these odes, however, is on the theme of fortune. The first two, however, are in the Second Asclepiadean meter.

Text:

7-10. The poet likens fortune to a crazily bouncing ball. The final version omits an earlier line, "It now will fly through quiet summer air."

11. *Vesper vespere truditur.* Horace wrote, *"Truditur dies die" Carm.* 2.18.15.

17. *essedo:* An *essedum* was a two-wheeled chariot of the Gauls and Britons. Afterwards, the Romans used the *essedum* for pomp and show in sham fights.

30 Eversis sepelit turribus oppida:
  Ac mundi procul arduas
   Stragesque et cumulos, ac procerum pyras
  Festa nube supervolat;
   Stellarumque rotam, et longa brevissimo
35 Cursu saecula corripit.
   Dum nobis taciti diffugiunt dies,
  Eheu! Telephe, ludimur,
   Fatorum rapida ludimur orbita.
  An nos fallimur? an suam
40   Rerum pulcher habet vultus imaginem?
  Et sunt quae, Lyce, cernimus?
   An peccant fatuis lumina palpebris,
  Et mendax oculi vitrum?
   An longi trahitur fabula somnii?

30   The wheeling stars, the years of mortal man,
       She closes off with all too speedy course.
          While silently our days are passing by,
       We are the sport of fate's quick changing acts.
          Or are we mocked? Does not creation's face
35   With her fair beauty hold divine design?
          Or do our eyes deceive us as we gaze
       Into the mirror of God's handiwork?
          Or are we only dreaming in the night,
       An idle dream of short enduring flight.

---

30. *years:* age;   32. *passing:* flitting;   39. *idle:* futile;   39. *flight:* night
39. *short:* long.

Poem 3

Liber II, Ode II
Ad Publium Memmium

Vitae humanae brevitatem benefactis extendendam esse

    Quae tegit canas modo bruma valles,
    Sole vicinos iaculante montes
    Deteget rursum. Tibi cum nivosae
        Bruma senectae

5   In caput seris cecidit pruinis,
    Decidet numquam. Cita fugit aestas,
    Fugit autumnus: fugient propinqui
        Tempora veris.

    At tibi frigus, capitique cani
10 Semper haerebunt: neque multa nardus,
    Nec parum gratum repetita dement
        Serta colorem.

    Una quem nobis dederat iuventus,
    Una te nobis rapiet senectus;
15 Sed potes, Publi, geminare magna
        Saecula fama.

    Quem sui raptum gemuere cives,
    Hic diu vixit. Sibi quisque famam
    Scribat heredem: rapiunt avarae
20   Cetera lunae.

Meter: Sapphic Strophe

Title: The addressee, Publius Memmius, is unknown. The brevity of earthly life is a common theme in the Jesuit Latin poets. As often, Mertz referred to his version as an "adaptation"; earlier it had the title, "Brevity of life to be prolonged by good deeds".

Poem 3

Book 2, Ode 2
To Publius Memmius

Life's brief span is stretched by goodness.

    The snows that chill the graying fields
    Will melt before the summer sun
        That warms the hills;

    But hoary locks will never yield
5   To youthful warmth, when years are done
        With all their thrills.

    The summer's heat to fall gives way,
    The winter's cold awaits the breath
        Of burgeoning spring;

10   But once your head is marked with gray,
    And years approach the time of death
        So harrowing –

    No secret nards will stop the harm,
    Nor bring the youthful warmth again
15   Into your face;

    For youth bestows but once her charm,
    While age will steal in secret pain
        All youthful grace.

    But you may build a newer life
20   Upon the hidden deeds of love
        Which God alone

    Will keep for you from all decay.
    All else will moulder fast away
        You thought your own.

Text:

1-8. Horace marshals the seasons at *Carmina* 4.7.9-12.

9. *cani:* is a substantive here, "white hair", "venerable age".

19. *rapiunt:* Some versions read *fugiunt* here.

19-20. *avarae lunae:* As at *Odes* I.4.2-3 (number 1) for "greedy, impatient moons". Mertz's translation/adaptation adds a religious thought that is not in Sarbiewski's poem.

Poem 4

Liber II, Ode III
Ad suam testudinem

Sonora buxi filia sutilis,
Pendebis alta, barbite, populo,
   Dum ridet aër, et supinas
      Sollicitat levis aura frondes.

5   Te sibilantis lenior halitus
    Perflabit Euri: me iuvet interim
      Collum reclinasse, et virenti
         Sic temere iacuisse ripa.

    Eheu! serenum quae nebulae tegunt
10 Repente caelum! quis sonus imbrium!
      Surgamus. Heu, semper fugaci
         Gaudia praeteritura passu!

---

1. *boxwood:* oaken; 3. *And...softly blow:* And while the winds sough thru the trees; 4. *The wakened...reply:* And echo forth the wakened leaves reply; 5. *The lightest breaths:* The slightest breath; 6. *melody:* melodies; 7. *Me pillowed:* Me lying pillowed; 8. *To mark your:* And listening to your.

Meter: Alcaic strophe

Title: "In sweet music is such art/Killing care and grief of heart" Shakespeare, *Henry VIII.* III.1.13-14.

Poem 4

Book 2, Ode 3
To His Lyre

Sweet-singing daughter of the boxwood reed,
   You'll hang aloft on poplar branches high,
And as the breezes softly blow, you'll heed
   The wakened rustling leaves in their reply.

5   The lightest breaths of East Wind's murmuring sigh
   Upon your strings with melody beguile
Me pillowed on the grasses nigh,
   To mark your pleasant music notes the while.

Alas! what clouds are marshaling in the sky!
10   The thunders roll, the rain is driving fast!
Oh, let's away – the fondest joys pass by
   On speedy wings, and all too brief to last.

Text:

1. *buxi:* a *buxus* is a pale evergreen box tree; a pipe or flute made from this wood.

1. *sutilis:* a derivative of *suo, suere* to sew, bind together.

2. *barbite:* a *barbitos* in a lyre or lute. See Horace *Carmina* 1.32.4, which is an invocation addressed to the poet's lyre.

Poem 5

Liber II, Ode X
Honesto otio addictus saeculi sui vitiis bellum indicit.

    Meo beatus, cetera vilibus
    Habere fatis, et miserabili
        Permitto vulgo: quos secundo
        Per populos vehat axe rumor,

5   Quem donet astris gloria, fortiter
    Ignarus: et quae lex sapientibus,
        Idem meas nescire, et idem
        A populo didicisse laudes,

    Latere clauso certior ostio:
10 At ne malignis fama calumniis
        Me iactet arcanum probrosis
        Flagitium simulare tectis,

    Audax vel ipso vivere publicus
    In sole civis. Non ego ludicrae
15   Dixi sacramentum Minervae
        Innocuus sine caede miles:

    Sed bellicoso strenuus ardui
    Amore veri crimina saeculi
        Fraudesque et indevota laudi
20   Pectora desidiamque frango

    Ultore versu. Quem nimis asperum
    Exsuscitando numina gentium
        Regem esse nolebant veterno,
        Esse tamen voluere vatem.

---

1. *all else:* everything; 1-2. *miserable mob:* dumb dorries *(sic)*; 2. *let...may:* their final issue; 9. *harms;* 13. *wanted:* have wished.

Meter: Alcaic strophe

Title: "Do not put me to it. For I am nothing if not critical." Shapespeare, *Othello* II.1.119-20.

Poem 5

Book 2, Ode 10

At leisure, the author declares war on the vices of his day.

    Content I go my way and leave all else to the miserable
mob – let the chips fall as they may!

    I am blissfully ignorant of all talk of advance in glory,
of praise I have won, and unmindful of any noised abroad.

5   I am safer in my own room with locked doors.
But to prevent idle talk from making me an object of blame,

    I have fully determined to live publicly in the eyes of all,
and have made my promise to Minerva, like a soldier,
    but without war's effects.

10   I'm always ready to fight the battle for truth,
and smash all pretense and idleness

    By my avenging verse. The one whom the gods did not wish
to be a king they wanted to be a poet.

Text:

15. *sacramentum:* a military oath of allegiance. Mertz's adaptation seems to miss the bellicose spirit of Sarbiewski in these verses. "War's effects" will be fully operative.

15. *Minervae:* goddess of war and of wisdom.

18. *amore veri:* this is a play on his old family name *Prawda,* which means, "truth". The last stanza is a reference to his own family which was of princely stock.

23. *veterno:* is a substantive here, "lethargy".

Poem 6

Liber II, Ode XV
Ad Narviam

Cuius in ripa puer admodum primum carmen lyricum cecinerat.

    Albis dormiit in rosis,
        Liliisque iacens et violis dies,
    Primae cui potui vigil
        Somnum Pieria rumpere barbito,
5   Curae dum vacuus puer
        Formosi legerem litora Narviae.
    Ex illo mihi posteri
        Florent sole dies: qui simul aureae
    Infregit radios lyrae,
10   Iam nec scuta sonat, nec strepitum trucis
    Gradivi; sed amabiles
        Ruris delicias: sive rubentia
    Udo rore rosaria,
        Seu molles violas, sive volubilem
15   Leni flumine Viliam,
        Seu primo graciles vere Favonios.
    At tu, Narvia, quem puer
        Tum primum Calabra personui fide,
    Ictu pectinis hoc habe
20   Incisum viridi carmen in ilice:
    Quem Phoebus citharae pater,
        Quem laetae citharis Pierides amant,
    Laetum barbita Narviam,
        Laetum virginei semper ament chori.

---

3. *arose:* rose; 19. *within:* with.

Meter: Second Asclepiadean system

Title: The Narvia is the Narew, a river is Masovia, Poland, a tributary of the Bug. The phrase *puer admodum* alludes to the fact that Sarbiewski wrote a poem in honor of the Narew when he was thirteen years old. An earlier title was, "On the Banks of His Native Stream When the Author was Thirteen Years Old".

Poem 6

Book 2, Ode 15
To Narvia

On whose bank the young poet sang his first song

    The day was sleeping in the rose,
        The lily white, and violet,
    When early in the morn I arose
        To lyric forth my triolet.

5   To sing in sweet Pierian song –
        As free from care, in boyish glee,
    I strolled thy beauteous banks along
        And gazed in rhapsody

    Into the future years to ring
10   With melodies I wrote that day,
    When on the golden lyre's string
        Thy groves reechoed to my lay.

    I did not sing of warrior's shield
        Or sound of dour soldier's march;
15   But of thy sylvan joys afield,
        Of flowers and trees and spreading larch.

    I sang of roses tinted red.
        Of violets blue, of Vilia's streams
    That babbling purled within their bed,
20   When first the West Wind called to dreams.

    Dear Narvia, thy praise shall last,
        Which I, the boy, in lyric way,
    Upon thy oaks carved deep and fast
        To last beyond my shorter day.

Text:

6. *legerem lítora:* I was wandering or walking along the shore.
11. *Gradivi:* a surname of Mars.
15. *Viliam:* the Viliya, a stream in Lithuania on which Vilna lies.
18. *Calabra...fide:* lyric poetry. It is called "Calabrian" since Ennius, the father of Latin literature, was born in ancient Calabria.

>   25 Haec, dum sponte virentia
>   Vivent in teneri vulnere corticis,
>   Addiscent pueri tibi,
>   Addiscent tacitae carmina virgines:
>   Festo mox eadem die,
>   30   Dum glebam solidae lucis et igneas
>   Electri lacrimas legent,
>   Partiti geminis litora coetibus,
>   Alternis pueri tibi,
>   Alternis recinent carmina virgines.

Text:

25ff. Another version of the closing lines of *Odes* 2.15 is:
>   And when my lyrics on that bark
>   Would wider grow in future years;
>   The boys and girls will come to hark
>   And sing of me with loving tears.

31. *legent:* here, "collect"

25   The oaks Apollo loved so well,
        And where the Muses, fond of song,
    Would gather in their shade to dwell
        And maids their roundelays prolong.

        The boys and girls in festive years,
30   Will gather in this native park
    To pick the resin-ambered tears,
        That hold the secret of my harp.

---

29. *in...years:* on...days.

Poem 7

Liber II, Ode XXV
Ex sacro Salomonis Epithalamio

Fulcite me floribus, stipate me malis, quia amore langueo.
Adiuro vos, filiae Ierusalem, ne suscitetis, neque evigilare
faciatis dilectam, quoadusque ipsa velit.
Ecce iste venit, saliens in montibus, transiliens colles.
Similis est Dilectus meus capreae, hinnuloque cervorum.
Canticum canticorum 2.5,7-9.

    Me stipate rosariis:
        Me fulcite crocis: me violariis,
    Me vallate cydoniis:
        Me canis, sociae, spargite liliis:
5   Nam visi mora Numinis
        Mi sacris animam torret in ignibus.
    Vos o, vos ego filiae
        Caelestis Solymae: vos Galaditides,
    Vos, o per capreas ego
10   Errantesque iugis hinnuleos, precor,
    Antiqui genus Isaci,
        Quae saltus Libani, quae viridem vago
    Carmelum pede visitis,
        Nymphae, nobilium gloria montium:
15 Ne vexate tenacibus
        Acclinem violis: neu strepitu pedum,
    Neu plausae sonitu manus
        Pacem solliciti rumpite somnii:
    Donec Sponsa suo leves

---

1. *surround me:* prop me up; 3. *lilies white:* Cana lilies; calla lilies; 8. *grazing:* wandering; 8. *heights:* ridges; 10. *old stock:* ancient stock; 14. *do not tramp along:* do not with the step of your feet; 14. *clap your hands:* clapping of hands.

Meter: Second Asclepiadean system

Title: Traditionally, this delicate love song is interpreted as expressing the spiritual love of Christ for the soul. It is full of oriental imagery. Such paraphrases of the Song of Songs and other texts were quite common in the 17th century Latin poets such as Urban VIII or Jacob Vande Walle.

Poem 7

Book 2, Ode 25
From the Song of Songs of Solomon

Surround me with flowers, refresh me with apples,
for I am faint with love. I adjure you,
daughters of Jerusalem, do not arouse,
do not stir up love before its own time.
Hark! my lover - here he comes springing
across the mountains, leaping across the hills.
My lover is like a gazelle or a young stag.

    Surround me with rose petals,
    With the crocus and the violet, the quince apple
    And lilies white;
    For the delay of my Lord whom I have seen
5   Has weighed down my soul with holy fire of love.
    You, O daughters of the heavenly Jerusalem,
    You, daughters of Galilee,
    I beg you by all the goats grazing on the heights
    And by all the fawns;
10   You, the old stock of Isaac,
    You who visit the ancient heights of Libanus
    And tread the green lawn of Carmel, glory of all mountains;
    Do not disturb him sleeping in the violets.
    No, do not tramp along or clap your hands,
15   Do not disturb his peaceful slumber
    Until my spouse wipe sleep from his eyes
    And the golden morning star wake him from rest.
    Behold, he is the son of a most beautiful mother;
    He is the only son of a most beautiful father.

Text:

3. *cydoniis:* quinces or quince apples.

8. *Solymae:* for the more common *Hierosolymae,* Jerusalem.

8. *Galaditides:* daughters of Galaad, a mountain and plateau connecting Lebanon and Syria; here *Galaditides* = Jewish maidens. Galaad is the biblical Gilead.

10. *hinnuleos:* harts, young stags.

11. *Libanus:* Mertz wrote this for the more usual "Lebanon". *Libanus* reflects the original Latin form.

13. *Carmelum:* a mountain in Galilee, covered with wild flowers.

13. *Lucifer:* the morning star, the planet Venus.

20   Somnos ex oculis pollice terserit:
        Donec Lucifer aureus
            Rerum paciferum ruperit otium.
        Summis ecce venit iugis
            Formosae suboles matris, et unica
25   Formosi suboles patris:
            Silvarumque super colla comantium, et
        Intonsum Libani caput,
            Magnorumque salit terga cacuminum, ac
        Proceras nemorum domos
30   Prono transiliens praeterit impetu:
        Veloci similis caprae,
            Quae visis humili in valle leonibus,
        Per praerupta, per ardua
            Sublimi volucris fertur anhelitu.

Text:

24. *unica: unicae* is a variant printed in some editions, but it is clearly incorrect, though it might represent an original *unice.*

25. *formosi suboles patris:* This is a reference to Christ, Son of a beautiful Father. In line 24 Sarbiewski alludes to Mary.

20 He is now coming, dancing over the wooded hills,
    Over the top of Libanus with its heights,
    Over the homes of the ancient race.
    He comes with haste,
    Like a gazelle, which has seen the lions in the valley,
25 With head erect is carried breathlessly to the heights.

Poem 8

Liber II, Ode XXVII
Ad Claudium Rufum
Sibi sepulcra et tumulos regum scholam esse

Non me Democriti sales,
    Non me Cecropii porticus atrii,
Non percussa docentium
    Delectant calidis pulpita iurgiis,
5 Vel quae pectoris impotens
    Clamosi celebrat turba Panaetii;
Vel quae Pythagorae senis
    Docta tusse crepant. Me veterum frequens
Memphis Pyramidum docet:
10 Me pressae tumulo lacrima gloriae:
Me proiecta iacentium
    Passim per populos busta Quiritium,
Et vilis Zephyro iocus
    iactati cineres, et procerum rogi,
15 Fumantumque cadavera
    Regnorum tacito, Rufe, silentio
Maestum multa monent. Mihi
    Pompei gelido sub Iove segreges
Artus, et lacrimae carens

---

4. *heated:* fiery; 5. *or:* even. 5. *bootless:* fruitless. 14. *and the ashes...jest:* and the idle jest of the wind that scatters the ashes. 16. *pyres:* piles. 24. *terse:* brief. 26. *He no longer...wealth:* who does not ask for regal wealth. 27. *I won't have to sweat:* I poor fellow would not sweat.

Meter: Second Asclepiadean system

Title: Mertz considered and rejected the titles, "A Walk through the Forum," and "Lessons Learned in a Walk through the Forum". For a caption he had suggested "The boast of heraldry and the pomp of power."

Poem 8

Book 2, Ode 27
To Claudius Rufus

Vain are the tombs and monuments of kings.

      Not for me the wit of Democritus,
         Not for me the porch of the halls of Cecrops,
      Not for me the desks of the teachers
         With their heated wranglings,
5   Or the bootless band
         Of loud-sounding Panaetius,
      Or even old Pythagoras
         With his learned hacking.
      Memphis with its many pyramids
10   Teaches me a tearful lesson
      Of glory that was;
      The graves of our nobles
      Scattered among the nations
         And the ashes scattered by the wind in idle jest,
15   And the corpses of kings
         On the funeral pyres –
      These teach a great lesson
         In quiet reflection.
      Picture for me the limbs

Text:

1. *Democriti:* Democritus was born at Abdera in Thrace in 460 B.C. Cf. Juvenal, *Satire* X.33: "He was ever laughing at the follies of mankind" *(perpetuo risu pulmonem agitare solebat)*. The laughing philosopher was contrasted with the "melancholy Heraclitus", who wept at man's folly *(Ibid.* 30).

2. *Cecropii:* Cecrops, the legendary ancestor of the first kings of Athens; he is a sort of Adam figure.

6. *Panaetii clamosi:* Panaetius, a noted Stoic philosopher, was born at Rhodes. His dates are c.180-110 B.C. He came to Rome and influenced Scipio, his followers, and Roman thought.

7. *Pythagorae:* Pythagoras was born at Samos around 580 B.C. He was a member of a school bound to asceticism in food, and received his doctrine at Delphi, as his name indicates. He taught the transmigration of souls, the numerical relation between the length of the strings on a zither and musical notes, and the origin of the world in vibration. It was he who determined that the square of the hypotenuse of a right triangle is equal to the sum of the squares of the other two sides. Later his doctrine was fused with Orphism in Rome.

18-19. *Pompei...artus:* Pompey's death became a symbol of the fall of the mighty. An earlier version reads, "You may separate for me the limbs."

20   Desertoque vagum litore funus, et
   Magni nominis indigum
      Corpus, magniloqui verba Panaetii
   Compensat brevius; neque
      Regales patitur quaerere copias.
25   Nolim Pieriis macer
      Insudare libris, aut tacito vigil
   Impallescere Socrati:
      Si regum titulos, et tumulis super
   Fulgentem premo gloriam, et
30   Calco nobilium nomina Caesarum.

20   Of Pompey lying under the open sky
   And with dry eyes look at the luckless
      Shore line and the corpse of the great man
   Treated so shamefully –
      What a terse contrast with the words
25   Of the loud-sounding Panaetius!
      He no longer strives for regal wealth.
   I won't have to sweat and strain
      Over poetic works or
   Lose my color studying Socrates at night,
30   If I spurn the titles of royalty and
   Trample under foot
      The glory inscribed on their tombs
   And despise the names of the noble Caesars.

Poem 9

Liber III, Ode IV
Ad Egnatium Nollium

Aequo semper rectoque animo adversus fortunae inconstantiam standum esse

    Sive te molli vehet aura vento,
    Sive non planis agitabit undis;
    Vince fortunam, dubiasque, Nolli,
        Lude per artes.

5   Riserit? vultum generosus aufer.
    Fleverit? dulci refer ora risu.
    Solus, et semper tuus esse quovis
        Disce tumultu.

    Ipse te clausam modereris urbem
10 Consul aut Caesar: quoties minantum
    Turba fatorum quatiens serenam
        Pectoris arcem.

    Cum leves visent tua tecta casus,
    Laetus occures: praeeunte luctu
15 Faustitas et Pax subeunt eosdem
        Saepe penates.

    Dextra sors omnis gerit hoc sinistrum,
    Quod facit molles: habet hoc sinistra
    Prosperum, quem nunc ferit, imminentes
20   Durat in ictus.

    Ille, qui longus fuit, esse magnus
    Desinit maeror. Facilem ferendo
    Finge fortunam: levis esse longo
        Discit ab usu.

---

2. *whips:* stirs; 3. *meet your lot:* meet each one with the same tenor of your way; 8. *in mob fashion:* like a mob; 14. *By bearing it...:* Imagine that fortune is easy to bear.

Meter: Sapphic strophe

Title: Mertz originally entitled his paraphrase, "Common Sense".

Poem 9

Book 3, Ode 4
To Egnatius Nollius

Keep the even tenor of your way even in adversity.

    If a gentle wind blows on you
    Or one that whips up the waves,
    Meet your lot and smile on fickle fortune.

    If fortune smiles on you, turn away your face;
5   If fortune weeps over you, meet her with a smile.

    Like a consul or a Caesar rule
    Your own heart, a fortified city,
    As often as the fates, in mob fashion, threaten to attack.

    If things are easy, meet them happily;
10 Prosperity and Peace meet before the same hearth.

    Success has this danger - it softens;
    Hard luck makes us ready for any event.

    Grief that has lasted long will come to an end;
    By bearing it, make fate seem easy; long use will make it so.

Text:

15. *Faustitas:* prosperity, personified as a goddess; so also *Pax*.

21. Cicereo wrote this succinct version of the Epicurean dictum on pain, *"Si gravis, brevis; si longus, levis"* (If grave, short; if long, slight), *De Finibus* 2.22.

Poem 10

Liber III, Ode XV
Ad apes Barberinas

Melleum venisse saeculum

Cives Hymetti, gratus Atticae lepos,
    Virgineae volucres,
    Flavaeque veris filiae,

Gratum fluentis turba praedatrix thymi,
5   Nectaris artifices,
    Bonaeque ruris hospitae,

Laboriosis quid iuvat volatibus,
    Crure tenus viridem
    Perambulare patriam,

10 Si Barberino delicata principe
    Saecula melle fluunt,
    Parata vobis saecula?

---

2. *progeny:* offspring; 9. *tread:* walk; 10. *flowered homeland:* country site; 11. *if:* when; 11. *age of:* age under; 12. *with the:* omitted; 13. *that will:* to.

Meter: Iambic trimeter and iambic dimeter surrounding a dactylic trimeter catalectic line. Horace does not use this metrical scheme. Stanzas composed of three different verses are quite exceptional.

Title: The crest of the Barberini has three golden flying bees on an argent background. Sarbiewski refers to this crest in a delicate poem he wrote on the accession of Matteo Barberini to the papal throne as Urban VIII on August 26, 1623.

Poem 10

Book 3, Ode 15
To the Barberini Bees

Coming of the Honeyed Age

    Dwellers of Hymettus, charm of Attica
        Virgin bee progeny,
    And golden daughters of Spring,

    Pirates of the rose and distillers of nectar,
5   Marauders of the mint,
    And pleasant guests of the meadows –

    What need to fly with beating wings
        Over countryside and fields,
    And tread with tired limbs
10   O'er flowered homeland,

    If the age of Barberini
        Flows with the delicate honey
    That will sweeten your years?

Text:

1. *Hymetti:* a mountain near Athens, famed for its honey.

4. Mertz's "Pirates of the rose" translates a variant reading *"Fures rosarum"*.

8-9. Mertz followed the variant reading, *"Rus et agros gravidis/Perambulare cruribus"*.

Poem 11

Liber IV, Ode XIV
Ad Crispum Laevinium

Rogatus, cur saepe per viam caneret, respondet.

    Cum meam nullis humeros onustus
    Sarcinis tecum patriam reviso
    Laetus, et parvo mihi cumque dives
        Canto viator;

5   Tu siles maestum: tibi cura Musas
    Demit, et multi grave pondus auri,
    Quaeque te quondam, malefida rerum,
        Turba relinquet.

    Dives est, qui nil habet; illa tantum
10 Quae potest certa retinere dextra:
    Seque fert secum, vaga quo migrare
        Iussit egestas.

    Quid mihi, qui nil cupiam, deesse
    Possit? Umbrosi placet una Pindi
15 Vallis, O sacrum nemus! O iocosae
        Rura Camenae!

    Quae meos poscet via cumque gressus,
    Delphici mecum, mea regna, colles
    Itis, et fessum comitante circum-
20   sistitis umbra.

    Me Gothus saevis religet catenis,
    Me Scythes captum rapiat, soluta
    Mente vobiscum potero tremendos
        Visere reges.

Meter: Sapphic strophe

Title: The addressee is perhaps the Lewinski with whom Sarbiewski traveled from Rome back to his homeland (see *Odes* I.4; number 1 in this collection.) An earlier English title of the piece was, "To his friend when asked why he sang so joyfully on the journey."

Poem 11

Book 4, Ode 14
To Crispus Laevinius
Why he sang so joyfully on his way

No heavy pack weighs on my back
    As home I make my way,
The songs I sing through woodlands ring,
    A traveler's joyous lay.

5   But worry's trace is on your face –
    The Muses note it well.
And all your gold and wealth untold
    Will miss their hearty spell.

He's rich indeed whose only need
10   Is what he holds in hand;
With that he'll well go forth to dwell
    Where want besets the land.

What can I miss whose only bliss
    Is nature's lovely rest,
15 Or sacred grove where I may rove
    And laugh in idle jest?

Whate'er the way I walk by day,
    And wearied though I be,
The greening hills will cast their thrills
20   And keep me company.

The Goth may bind and Moor unkind
    May capture me – and still,
With your kind grace, dear Muse, I'll face
    An angry monarch's will.

Text:

14. *Pindi:* the Pindus, a lofty mountain on the borders of Macedonia and Epirus. It was sacred to Apollo and the Muses. Today it is called Mexara.

18. *Delphici colles:* Parnassus, home of the Muses.

Poem 12

Liber IV, Ode XVIII
Ad rosam

Quotannis Kalendis Iunii D. Virginis caput coronaturus

    Siderum sacros imitata vultus,
    Quid lates dudum, rosa? delicatum
    Effer e terris caput, o tepentis
        Filia caeli.

5   Iam tibi nubes fugiunt aquosae,
    Quas fugant albis Zephyri quadrigis;
    Iam tibi mulcet Boream iocantis
        Aura Favoni.

    Surge: qui natam deceant capilli,
10 Mitte scitari: nihil, heu, profanae
    Debeas fronti, nimium severi
        Stemma pudoris.

    Parce plebeios redimire crines,
    Te decent arae: tibi colligenda
15 Virginis late coma per sequaces
        Fluctuat auras.

---

5. *drifted:* lifted; 6. *in:* is; 7. *wind:* blast; 7. *icy winds:* icy chill; 7. *of icy winds sifted:* which icy winds lifted; 8. *joyous the West Wind:* by playing West Wind; 14. *thou'lt share:* to share.

Meter: Sapphic strophe

Title: An alternate title is, "Crowning of our Lady's statue on June 1".

Poem 12

Book 4, Ode 18
To the Rose

On every first of June the statue of Mary is crowned.

    Sweet rose reflecting the star mantle luster,
        Why art thou hiding when summer is nigh?
    Lift from earth's bosom thy flowery cluster,
        Child of the warm sun now riding on high.

5   The Zephyrs are blowing, the rain clouds have drifted,
        Scattered afar in their dark argosy;
    Warmed is the North Wind, of icy winds sifted,
        Joyous the West Wind now calling on thee.

    Rise with the spring bloom, Oh, cease thy beguiling,
10   No worldly trapping is needed for thee;
    Wafting thy perfume and the blush of thy smiling
        Modest thou'lt be for my deep reverie.

    Not for a corsage o'er woman's heart beating!
        A place on the altar of Mary thou'lt share,
15   Where with thy beauty thou'lt give here my greeting
        As she will lift thee to place in her hair.

Text:

10. *scitari:* to seek to know. It is a poetic and mostly late Latin word. Cicero used *sciscitari*. Also, Sarbiewski echoes Horace, *Carmina* I.38.3: *Mitte sectari, rosa quo locorum/sera moretur.*

Poem 13

Liber IV, Ode XIX
Ad Iesum Opt. Max.
Ex sacro Salomonis Epithalamio

Indica mihi, quem diligit anima mea,
ubi pascas, ubi cubes in meridie. (Cant. I.6)

    Dicebas abiens: Sponsa vale; simul
    Vicisti liquidis nubila passibus.
        Longam ducis, Iesu,
           In desideriis moram.

5   Ardet iam medio summa dies polo:
    Iam parcit segeti messor, et algidas
        Pastor cum grege valles,
           Et pictae volucres petunt.

    At te quae tacitis distinet otiis,
10   O Iesu, regio? quis mihi te locus
        Caecis invidet umbris,
           Aut spissa nemorum coma?

    Scirem, quo iaceas caespite languidus!
    Quis ventus gracili praeflet anhelitu!
15   Quis rivus tibi grato
           Somnum praetereat sono!

    Ah! ne te nimio murmure suscitent,
    Nostrae diluerent flumina lacrimae,
        Et suspiria crudis
20   Miscerentur Etesiis.

---

2. *speedy:* hasty; 3. *You caused...:* you gave my heart's love a long delay; 5. *guards his flock:* leads his flock; 8. *of the dark:* or the dark; 11. *which stream:* some stream; 13. *hasty in waking you:* long in resting you.

Meter: Alcaic strophe

Title: There is a certain amount of mysticism in the manner of Francis Thompson. Four main loves are detected in the writing of Sarbiewski: love for the crucified Son of God, for his own country, for the mother of our Lord, and for nature or God's creation.

Poem 13

Book 4, Ode 19
To Jesus the Greatest Good
(From the Song of Songs of Solomon)

Tell me, you whom my heart loves, where you pasture your flock, where you give them rest at midday. (Cant. I.6)

    As you departed you kept on saying: Farewell, my spouse,
      farewell!
    Immediately, dear Jesus, you rose over the clouds with
      speedy feet.
    You caused great longing in my heart.
    Midday is hot with the sun high in the sky;
5   The farmer quits the field; the shepherd who guards his flock
    Makes for the cool valley as do the mottled birds.
    But where are you, dear Jesus?
    Hidden in some leafy shade of the dark shadows of a grove?
    I would like to know where you rest on some green hill,
10   Or what wind kindly blows over you,
    Or which stream lulls you to sleep with its murmuring.
    Oh, if only they would not be too hasty in waking you.
    Would that my tears could build into streams!
    Would that my longings could touch you with gusts of wind
      from the East!

Text:

12. *aut spissa nemorum coma:* Sarbiewski echoes Horace, *Carm.* 4.3.11: *et spissae nemorum comae.* Verse 14 echoes *Carm.* 1.5.4: *Quis multa gracilis.*

20. *Etesiis:* "yearly" winds, Trade Winds.

Poem 14

Liber IV, Ode XXIII
Ad cicadam

    O quae, populea summa sedens coma,
    Caeli roriferis ebria lacrimis,
        Et te voce, cicada,
            Et mutum recreas nemus.

5   Post longas hiemes, dum nimium brevis
    Aestas se levibus praecipitat rotis,
        Festinos, age, lento
            Soles excipe iurgio.

    Ut se quaeque dies attulit optima,
10 Sic se quaeque rapit: nulla fuit satis
        Umquam longa voluptas;
            Longus saepius est dolor.

---

2. *wet with sky's dewey tear:* drunk with dew-laden tear.

Meter: Fourth Asclepiadean system

Poem 14

Book 4, Ode 23
To the Cicada

    O thou on poplar high
        Wet with sky's dewey tear,
    Who with thy chirping cry
        Wak'st the mute grove to hear,

5   Now that winter's flown,
        Ere short-lived summer's done
    And days have shorter grown,
        Sing to the speeding sun!

    As each day brings its grace
10   And takes it back again –
    No pleasure keeps apace
        With sorrow's deeper pain.

Text:

Fr. Lawrence Braceland, S.J., a correspondent of Fr. Mertz, wrote this translation of *Odes* IV.23:

    Smart little cricket perched on high
    Drunk with the cheering dew!
    Morning's silence echoes the cry
    That brings a message from you.

    Long winter is passed and summer is here,
    Fast in its fall-ward race,
    Can't you persuade the thoughtless year
    To leave us summer's rare grace?

    Too few the days that pass along
    Bright under sun-lit sky!
    Too swift the hour of pleasure's song
    While endless rings woe's plaintive cry.

Poem 15

Liber Epodon, II
Ad fontem Sonam

In patrio fundo, dum Roma rediisset

    Fons innocenti lucidus magis vitro,
        Puraque purior nive,
    Pagi voluptas, una Nympharum sitis,
        Ocelle natalis soli,
5   Longis viarum languidus laboribus,
        Et mole curarum gravis
    Tuscis ab usque gentibus redux, tibi
        Accline prosterno latus.
    Permitte siccus, qua potes, premi; cava
10   Permitte libari manu,
    Sic te quietum nulla perturbet pecus,
        Ramusve lapsus arbore:
    Sic, dum loquaci prata garritu secas,
        Et laetus audiri salis,
15   Assibilantes populetorum comae
        Ingrata ponant murmura
    Tibi, lyraeque vatis. Haud frustra sacer
        Nam si quid Urbanus probat,
    Olim fluenti lene Blaudusiae nihil,
20   Aut Sirmioni debeas.

---

7. *while resting...*: as resting on thy brink, I sense thy calm; 8. *sheep:* kine; 9. *your silent sleep:* that silence thine; 9. *of sunshine free:* with laughter free; 10. *you flow:* thou flowest.

Meter: Iambic strophe (alternating trimeter and dimeter as in Horace, *Epodes* 1)

Title: As often, Mertz called his version an adaptation rather than a translation.

Poem 15

Book of Epodes, 2
To the Fountain, Sona

He revisits the fountain on his father's estate.

    Fountain so crystal clear, purer than snow,
        Charm of my village dear, where youth would go
    Thirsting to be more near your limpid flow,

    Wearied and travel-worn, laden with care,
5   I now return forlorn from Tuscan fare,
    Longing for one deep drink in hollowed palm,
        While resting on your brink, I sense your calm.

    May never strolling sheep nor falling tree
        Trouble your silent sleep of sunshine free;
10 And when with babbling peace you flow along,
        May the tall poplars cease their murmuring song.

    As bard I'll sing your lay ever more sweet,
        For in your waters play all charms replete.

Text:

7. *redux:* Sarbiewski returned from Rome in 1625 where he had been ordained after three years of theological studies and had taken part in the revision of the breviary hymns.

19. *Blaudusiae:* is the reading in all the printed editions I have been able to consult; but surely the standard *Bandusiae* is correct. *Blandusiae* is the reading of a large number of Horatian MSS at *Carmina* 3.13.1. Sarbiewski and subsequent editors must have been misled by it to read *Blaudusiae.* The first *u* may be a consequence of a common printing error in old books: a letter is set upside down: the correct *n* was set as the incorrect *u*.

21. *Sirmioni:* Sarbiewski alludes to Catullus who had a villa on Lake Garda in Northern Italy.

Poem 16

Liber Epodon, IV
De Puero Iesu
In Virginis Matris sinu

    Amemus. An Massylus, aut nostris riget
        Alpinus in venis silex?
    Amemus. En, ut pronus e Matris sinu
        In nostra pendet oscula;
5   Qualis severa vel Gelonorum puer
        Mollire posset pectora!
    Ut lumen oris, ut renidentes genas,
        Ut bina frontis sidera,
    Nivesque colli, quasque purus et tener
10   Titan inauravit comas,
    Eburneasque tendit in collum manus!
        Ut annuit totus rapi!
    Ut hospitali vagit admitti sinu,
        Stringique bracchiis rogat!
15   Amemus: aut si non amare possumus,
        Repente possimus mori.

---

2. *Afric's:* Africa's; 12. *charm:* charms.

Meter: Iambic trimeter and dimeter

Poem 16

Book of Epodes, 4
To the Boy Jesus

On the lap of the Virgin Mary

    Oh, let us love! Or have we harder grown
        Than Alpine crag or Afric's flintier stone?
    Oh, let us love! Inviting us to rest
        And share our kiss, he leans from Mary's breast.
5   Behold his charming smile and glowing grace,
        And all the tender beauty of his face:
    The starlight in his eyes, the neck so white,
        The curling locks endued with golden light.
    His ivory-tinted hands stretched out to me
10   To be embraced and his alone to be,
    He bids me open wide my heart and arms,
        That to my colder love he add his charm.
    Oh, let us love, or if in love we fail,
        Then let us die for what does life avail?

Text:

1. *Massylus:* Of the Massyli, a people of Africa; poetic for African, with the sense of 'barbarous'.

5. *Gelonorum:* the Geloni, a Scythian people in the modern Ukraine. The word has the same connotation as *Massylus*.

5-6. Sarbiewski echoes Horace, *Epod.* 5.13-14: *quale posset...mollire...pectora*.

10. *Titan:* son of Hyperion; the Sun-god.

Poem 17

Silviludium, II
Ad rorem

Saltus pastorum, cum Vladislaus Solecznikis mane venatum prodiret

I.

Placidi rores matutini,
Qui sereno lapsi caelo
  Mollia florum
  Versicolorum
5 Ocellatis folia;
Qui florentibus in conchis
  Late virentis
Aequore prati gemmulatis;

II.

Vigiles hortis ab Eois,
10 Florae rores olitores,
  Arida pratis
  Ora rigatis
Urnulis argenteis.
Vos Aurorae fulgurantis
15 Tacitus imber,
Guttulae caeli desudantis.

III.

Nitidum flavae lac Matutae,
Cum luteolas papillas
  Tenero florum
20 Inserit ori,
Odorati pupuli
Coloratis cum labellis
  Rosae circum
Ubera matris nutriuntur.

---

6. *Like:* with; 6. *the petal:* petalled; 7. *dips:* drips; 14. *sunracked:* brightening.

Meter: The meter is accentual. The predominant foot is the trochee, although lines 3, 4, and 7 of each stanza scan as adonics. The first and last lines of many stanzas also begin with an adonic; other stanzas begin, quantitatively, with an anapaest and spondee.

Title: John Sparrow in two studies published in the *Oxford Slavonic Papers* has proved conclusively that the *Silviludia* are not Sarbiewski's work. Instead, they are but slight modifications of Mario Bettini, S.J.'s *Ludovicus: Tragicum Silviludium*. Thus the pieces are pastoral drama, a genre foreign to Sarbiewski's poetic genius. The Sparrow studies are in Vol. 8 (1958) 1-48 and Vol. 12 (1965) 80-93.

  Soleczniki is a city between Vilna and Grodno. Mertz had an alternate title: "A hunting Song - early in the morning".

Poem 17

Silviludium, 2
To the Dew

Vladislaus goes hunting early in the morning at Soleczniki.

I.

You dews of morn,
So softly fallen from the skies,
   In silvery light
   And sunlight bright,
5   You sparkle with a thousand eyes
     Like pearls alight on the petal lips
     Each newly wakened flower dips
   On meadow bourne.

II.

Now called from sleep
10   The guardian of the eastern fields
     On arid wold
     Pours gifts untold,
   And silvery cups their moisture yield.
   Like silent rain from sun-racked sky
15   Tithonia's dewdrops iridescent lie
     On meadow deep.

III.

The snow-white milk
Fresh gathered on the breast of dawn
   Gives nourishment
20   And quickening scent
To flowery lips that sprinkle all the lawn;
   And clustered roses in all colors dressed
   Their perfume heap upon Aurora's breast
     Of airy silk.

Text:
3-4. Mertz: once translated these lines, *"With every hue/On leaf and rue."*
7. *virentis:* Some editions read *viretis*.
21. *odorati pupuli:* A variant reading is *odoratis populi*.

IV.

25　Stellulae noctis decedentis,
　　Stillae rorum, caeli rores,
　　　　Sidera ruris,
　　　　Sidera rores,
　　Flosculorum lacrimae,
30　Cum madenti liquent ore,
　　　　Diraque lugent
　　Funera noctis occidentis.

V.

　　Antra petentum vos ferarum
　　Pressa vago signa pede,
35　　　Limite fido
　　　　Prodite, rores.
　　Certa per vestigia
　　Ad latentem venatores
　　　　Ducite praedam,
40　Placidi rores matutini.

Text:
25. *decedentis:* Some editions read *decidentis.*

IV.

25 Like stars agleam
    Athwart the breaking light
        The dewy sheen
        On meadow green
    Betrays the tears that come with dying night;
30   And as they weep the night's demise
      So with newborn day they rise
        In sunlight's beam.

V.

    You dews of morn,
    Be guides to hunters after booty bent;
35   Betray the lair
      Of quarry fair,
    And guide their footsteps on the scent.
      Send forth the game; give all the thrill
      That every hunter's heart will fill
40   Come blow the horn! You dews of morn!

38-40: Omitted in some versions.

Poem 18 - Epigrams

Epigramma 16
D. Magdalena sub cruce flens

Ah sitio! clamas: absunt his rupibus undae;
  Sola fluunt oculis flumina, sola bibe.

Epigramma 18
Fortis est ut mors dilectio
Canticum canticorum 8.6

Ut scires, quo, Christe, tui flammarer amore
  Non unus pro me nuntius ivit amor.
Cor ad te misi; cor non est, Christe, reversum;
  Mitto voluntatem, Christe; nec illa redit.
5 Ut tandem totam posset tibi dedere mentem,
  Intellectus erat missus; et ille manet.
Nunc animam mitto: quod si non illa redibit,
  O ego quam vivum, Christe, cadaver ero!

Epigramma 33
Donec aspiret dies, et inclinentur umbrae
Canticum canticorum 2.17

Quid nocti lumen, luci quid quaerimus umbram?
  Nocte dies nobis est Amor, umbra die.

Epigramma 40
Veni de Libano, Sponsa.
Canticum canticorum 4.8

Et fugis, et fugiens clamas: Quid, Sponsa, moraris?
  Non fugis, ut fugias: ut capiare, fugis.

Meter: Elegiac distich

Title: Sarbiewski wrote 265 epigrams. They treat of all sorts of people–cardinals, bishops, priests, lay persons. They give us a good picture of his contemporaries, and the circumstances of time and place in which he lived. St. Aloysius Gonzaga and the *Canticle of Canticles* inspire very many epigrams. Horace did not write any epigrams that have come down to us and, therefore, is not Sarbiewski's model in these poems. The elegiac poets and the epigrammatist Martial are his models here.

Poem 18 - Epigrams

Epigram 16
Magdalene weeps beneath the cross

You cry, "I thirst": no waters flow from stone;
　The tears that flood my eyes–drink these alone.

Epigram 18
Love is as strong as death
Song of Songs 8.6

That you may know, dear Christ, how I would love
　I've often sent You messages above.
My heart I gave –it never was returned,
　My will I sent, with love it always burned.
5　To give my mind which you would keep your own
　My intellect I sent, in wisdom grown
And now my soul I give; if you retain
　How like a living corpse will I remain!

Epigram 33
Until day fades and shadows fall

　Why do we seek at night the light,
　　Why in the day the shade?
　Your love by right is light by night
　　By day our comfort made.

Epigram 40
Come from Lebanon, my bride.

　You flee, my spouse, and fleeing cry,
　　"Pray tell, why do you tarry?"
　You do not flee to pass me by,
　　But fly to be my quarry.

Text:

Epigram 18: This poem is inspired by the *Suscipe (Take and Receive)*, a favorite prayer of St.Ignatius even if not his composition.

Epigram 40: Variants of the final line are, "But that you may be my quarry", and "But wait to be my quarry".

Poem 18 - Epigrams

Epigramma 64
Ad Cosmicum de Quincto

Mulum Quinctus emit, sed caecum, Cosmice, mulum.
Unum oculum mulus non habet: ille duos.

Epigramma 118
In Philippum rhetorem

Non poterat iussus tria dicere verba Philippus:
Si vultis causam nosse, disertus erat.

Poem 18 - Epigrams

Epigram 64

To Cosmicus on Quinctus

Dear Cosmic hear, our Quinctus bought
    An ass completely blind
And Quinctus with two eyes to watch
    The bigger ass you'll find.

Epigram 118

Against Philip the rhetor

Where bade to speak our Philip failed
    Not three words could he utter.
You wish to know the reason why?
    He was too glib to stutter.

Text:

Epigram 64: Mertz used the approximate forms of the names in his English translations. He preferred something modern when the Latin suggested that to him (for example, *Laurus* suggested "Larry" to him.)

It is natural to read *luscum* (one-eyed) for *caecum,* but all editions read the latter. In the Latin of the humanists, *caecus* is used often for "partially blind", "one-eyed". *Luscus* was probably felt to be a term of abuse.

LIBER TERTIVS. SOCIETAS AGENS. 469

Scholæ altiorum scientiarum.

Diuinæ Palladis ædes.

Scientiarum præses & arbitra,
  Idea recti, candida Veritas,
  Delapsa cælo, Cherubini
    Numquid adest agitata pennis?
Adest, & ardet sub penetralibus,
Loiola, vestris degere, commodas
  Hic nacta sedes, quando IESV
    Luce videt radiare postes.
Videre magnos hic videor Sophos,
Et plena multo pectora numine,
  Rerumque naturæque fontes
    Ausa adytis penetrare apertis.
Regina cunctas sed supereminet

Letters prepare for Philosophy and Theology

Johannes Kreihing
(1595-1670)

Johannes Kreihing was born at Deventer in Overijssel, the Netherlands, on January 8, 1595. He entered the Upper Rhine province of the Society of Jesus on August 5, 1616 at the age of 21. In addition to his knowledge of Latin, Kreihing also had Greek and Hebrew. He served as rector at Bamberg (1635) and Erfurt (1646). He served as confessor to the Elector of Mainz. He died at Würzburg on April 27, 1670.

Kreihing collected and published a number of his poems in July, 1658. The work, under the title *Poemata aposcholasmatica (Poems from School Exercises)* is dedicated to the then recently elected emperor, Leopold I (Holy Roman Emperor 1658-1705). The six books of this collection are divided as follows: three books of epigrams, two books of elegies, and one book of miscellaneous poems. Kreihing also wrote in German a catechism on fasting (1653), participated in a project of setting the Sunday epistles and gospels to German verse and music, and published an emblem book entitled *Emblemata Ethico-Politica* (Antwerp, 1651).

Among other classical models, Kreihing copied the literary form of Propertius. Kreihing's style, in turn, was imitated by Sidronius De Hossche (1596-1650) and Willem Becanus (Van der Beke or Verbeke) (1608-1660). De Hossche became a master of form, meter, and purity of poetic diction, surpassing both Balde and Sarbiewski due to the teaching of Kreihing whose elegies are without the license which even more classical authors allow. In his quiet flow of diction, Kreihing equals Tibullus, Propertius, and Ovid, the classics of elegy. He also imitated Martial with numerous epigrams, and he even attempted Pindaric heights, including some Greek verse.

Poem 19

Epigrammatum Liber I, CVII
Anglia moderna

Anglia iudiciis scelerata, et caede nefanda,
    Perfida perpetuis Anglia digna probris;
Anglia sacrorum mactatrix improba Regum,
    Quaeque tui Domini sanguine foeda mades;
5   Aspice, quam iusta Numen trutinata bilance
    Dira latrocinii pensitet acta tui.
Quae regem interimis proprium, subiecta Tyranno es,
    Sceptraque iam non Rex, sed latro turpis habet.
Libera tu fieri voluisti; libera non es:
10   Pro Domino servus iam tua colla premit.
Leniter a vero tangi te Rege dolebas;
    Nunc tua deglubit tergora vilis homo.
Praefata es Pacem, ast accenderis undique bello,
    Arma foris tibi sunt; cura, metusque domi!
15   Ursisti missis dissolvi signa maniplis
    Cum Regi exiguo tempore miles erat;
Milite perpetuo sed nunc, quasi capta, teneris;
    Arma opus in promptu namque Tyrannus habet.
Dissidii libuit tibi nunc praetexere causam,
20   Quod redeat veteris Religionis amor;
At nunc in toto tantum est confusio regno,
    Nullaque Religio certa, nec ulla fides,
Anglia quin oculis tandem es visura receptis?
24   Regina antea eras, nunc famuli famula es.

Meter: Elegiac distich

Title: Kreihing chides England for the execution of Charles I in 1649. The state of unrest that the poem depicts was the fighting done by Oliver Cromwell to suppress the Royalists.

Poem 19

Book 1, Epigram 107
England Today

 Profaned England! In all courts you stand guilty of everlasting reproach. Perfidious Albion! butcher of anointed kings and now stained with the blood of your own sovereign. Stop and think how justly God will judge your terrible robbery. (5) You, who execute your own king, are now subject to a tyrant. No king carries the scepter of authority at the present time; but a hated bandit is in command. You wanted to be free; you have lost the freedom you once had. (10) In the place of a good Lord, a slave rules over you. You suffered only slightly when the legitimate king ruled; now a criminal forges the chains he puts round your neck. You promised peace; but all about you are rumors of wars and at home there is nothing but fear and worry. (15) You forced the issue of liberty; now you are a captive forever. You wanted a separation and proposed this as reason. Would that the love of the ancient faith returned! (20) Now there is confusion, there is no faith, there is no religion. England, will you not open your eyes to see? Queen you once were, but now subservient to a slave.

Text:

 4. Kreihing echoes Virgil, *Aen.*12.690-91: *plurima fuso/Sanguine terra madet.*

 4. *Domini:* Charles I, who reigned from 1625 to 1649.

 5. *trutinata:* Both *trutino* and *trutinor* are attested. Because of the meter and sense (the passive voice is needed), the form here should be taken as the perfect passive participle of the first verb.

 12. *deglubit:* literally, "peal off, shell, husk," then, "skin, flay."

 12. *tergora:* collateral form of *terga,* backs.

 18. *Arma opus...habet:* Although rare, *opus habere* can mean "to have need of" and is construed with the ablative. Here it is obviously construed with the accusative and the sentence means, "The Tyrant has need of arms." An alternative explanation of *opus* is that it is in apposition to *arma,* which is object of *habet.* Thus the meaning would be, "The Tyrant has weapons, a thing that is obvious" *(opus in promptu).*

 19. *Dissidii:* variant spelling of *discidii.*

Poem 20

Epigrammatum Liber II, LII
De hiemis adventu, et frigore corporis humani

En horret gelidus saevis Aquilonibus aether,
    Et iacet effusa terra sepulta nive.
Non viror est herbis, non laetis gratia campis,
    Arboreasque comas cana recidit hiems.
5   Fumida perculsos reparant hypocausta calores;
    Et facit aestatem, quam negat aura, focus.
Condita iam tectis, suspenso segnis aratro,
    Vulcano frangit rustica turba gelu:
Hic sedet ad prunas, vestes sibi duplicat alter,
10   Quique caret, flatu calfacit ille manus.
Frigora sic miseris, atque algida bruma, timentur,
    Quique domat Scythicus corpora lenta rigor.
Ast ea, qua stygia mens infestatur ab Arcto,
    Heu vix sentitur, quin et amatur hiems;
15   Hic neque Sarmatico quaeruntur ab aequore pelles
    Daca nec hirsuto vellere fulta toga:
Nec curae est calido flamma crepitante camino
    Ingerere aggesta fervida ligna strue.
Sed quasi congenitis rigeant praecordia crustis,
20   Frigoris ab omni pectore sensus abest.
Pigra sub accensis durat salamandra favillis,
    Nativum medio nec perit igne gelu;
Sic sumus: admotis refovemus corpora flammis;
    Cordis at in calido corpore vivit hiems.
25   Corde carent homines; abiit de pectore centrum
    Pro corde in nobis iam salamandra sedet.

---

1. *chilled:* cold; 6. *denied to all:* to all denied; 16. *he buys:* are bought, does buy; 19. *fire burning:* burning fire, fire a burning. 20. *interlaced:* intertwined; 21. *bodies:* feelings.

Meter: Elegiac distich

Title: An alternate English title was the "Cold Winter Days".

Poem 20

Book 2, Epigram 52

Winter comes and the human body freezes.

    The air is chilled with the North Wind's icy blasts;
        The once green fields are buried deep in snow.
    The charm of blooming summer trees is lost,
        All leafless victims of bleak winter's frost.
5   And bellied stoves, red hot, pour out their smoke
        To challenge summer heat denied to all.
    The plough hangs high on peg within the shed,
        And farmer folk replenish blazing hearths.
    One sits and dozes in the warmer room,
10   Another piles on clothing in the chill,
    And one keeps blowing on his hands for warmth.
    The winter colds and icy days are feared,
        As Caspian blasts break down resisting strength.
    But one whose life matured in Northern clime,
15   Where cold is scarce perceived and even loved,
        No heavy pelts he buys in Sarmat land,
    No quilted clothes with fur from Danube land.
        No care is had to stack the furnace high,
    With logs to keep the fire burning bright.
20   As though their lives were interlaced with ice
    Their bodies do not seem to sense the cold.
    The fabled salamander lives in ashes hot,
        And does not perish in the fire's glow.
    We too rewarm our colder hearts with love,
25   Where listless care has taken full control.

Text:

3. *viror:* green color, greenness, verdure; it is post-classical for *viriditas,* which cannot be used in a dactylic verse.

13. *stygia mens:* Besides the name of a river in the infernal regions, *Styx* was also the name of a fountain in Arcadia. Its icy-cold water caused death.

21. *salamandra:* Pliny (*N.H.* 10.188) tell us *"Huic (salamandrae) tantus rigor ut ignem tactu restinguat non alio modo quam glacies."* (The salamander is so hard that it puts out fire by its touch not otherwise than ice does.) In the Middle Ages the myth grew that the salamander was fire-resistant from this classical view of the salamander as fire-extinguisher. Pliny also tell us that the salamander was highly poisonous.

Poem 21

Epigrammatum Liber II, LXII
De febri sua, et medico

En male, continuo numquam lassata recursu,
    Me coquit ardenti decolor igne febris:
Usque gelu, et saevos alternat flamma calores,
    Atque in me bellum frigus et aestus habent.
5   Guttura sicca sitis calidis vorat ignea prunis,
    Ambrosios stomacho sed regerente cibos;
Viribus exhaustis languor mihi degravat artus,
    Et manus afflictum vix levat aegra caput.
Fractaque nec teneros tolerant mea corpora lectos,
10   Sed pigro insomnes volvimur usque toro.
Nec tamen a medico capit ulla levamina morbus:
    Sed quotiens visor "non morieris" ait.
Iamque haec, dicta mihi toties, est cantio febris:
    Non peto ne moriar namque; sed ut valeam.

---

4. *chill:* heat; 5. *revolts:* is closed; 10. *no relief:* nothing; 10. *with the M.D.'s help:* from the doctor's help.

Poem 21

Book 2, Epigram 62

His fever and his doctor

    A sad story! the fever without letting up is doing me in!
        First a chill and then a flash of heat,
    Cold and heat are fighting it out in me.
        My throat is as dry as dust in the intermittent chill.
5   My stomach revolts and rejects the finest food;
        With strength gone my limbs are weak.
    My hand can hardly hold my pounding head;
        My aching body finds the softest mattress hard.
    I keep rolling on the bed without sleep;
10   The sickness gets no relief with the M.D.'s help.
    As often as he visits me he says, "You won't die."
        His one expression is supposed to be a cure.
    I am not asking not to die,
        But asking only to get well.

Meter: Elegiac distich

Title: A fuller title was, "The author's fever and his medical doctor".

Poem 22

Epigrammatum Liber III, LI
Sancta Monica ad Sanctum Augustinum filium

    Bis tibi sum genetrix, nam bis tibi luminis auras,
        Bisque tibi vitae munera grata dedi.
    Sed prior infaustum fecit mihi partus abortum
        Cum tibi corrupit faex Manichaea fidem.
5   Tunc ego te flebam noctes lacrimosa, diesque;
        Nec siccas habui tempora multa genas.
    O, quoties mundo me te peperisse dolebam!
        Nam mihi eras miserae mortuus atque Deo;
    Tunc ego cuncta meo madefeci altaria fletu;
10   Estque tibi lacrimis vita reducta meis.
    Sic ego bis genetrix, bis te quoque vivere feci,
        Et partu, et lacrimis; tunc mihi moxque Deo
    Et licet ob causam Mater tibi dicar utramque
        Plus tamen, ab lacrimis sum tibi facta, parens.

1. *I am:* am I; 1. *twice I gave:* twice did I give; 11. *I gave life...tears:* I gave you new life in my tears; 12. *and my life:* and life is mine; 12. *will soon go:* soon to be given; 13. *is so by a:* speaks a; 14. *your parent the more:* all the more your parent.

Meter: Elegiac distich

Poem 22

Book 3, Epigram 51
St. Monica to her son, St. Augustine

    Twice I am your mother, for twice I gave you light of day;
        Twice did I give you the gifts of life.
    The first birth was unhappy,
        For the Manichean heresy destroyed it.
5   I then wept for you night and day
        And my cheeks were not dry at any time.
    Oh, how often have I sorrowed to have given birth to you,
        For you died to me and to God.
    Bitterly I cried at the altar,
10   And life was given back by my tears.
    So I am twice your mother - I gave life by birth and by tears,
        And my life will soon go to God.
    And though your mother is so by a twofold cause,
        I am your parent the more by my tears.

Text:

3. *fecit...abortum:* miscarried, suffered abortion.

4. *faex Manichaea:* Augustine was a Hearer of the Manichaens from 374 A.D. for nine years (*Confessions* III.20). Augustine's baptism occurred still later than the nine years in 387 A.D.

9. *madefeci altaria fletu:* Monica prayed for her son's conversion for 33 years.

Title Page of 1634 Edition

Bernard Van Bauhuysen
(1575-1619)

Bernard Van Bauhuysen was born in Antwerp in modern Belgium on October 9, 1575. He entered the Society of Jesus in April, 1593 and became a professor of humanities. He decided to leave the teaching profession to devote his life to preaching, at which he enjoyed success. He died with a reputation for holiness and humility at Antwerp on November 17, 1619 at the age of 44.

Van Bauhuysen's poetic work in Latin consists of five books of epigrams. They were first published in 1616 at Antwerp. The poems in this edition and in several later seventeenth-century printings appear in combination with poems of other Jesuit Latin poets. For example, Malapert's poetry is published in its entirety in the 1616 Antwerp edition of Van Bauhuysen's work. The 1634 Antwerp edition also contains the epigrams of Bidermann and Malapert's poetry once again. Another Jesuit poet associated with Van Bauhuysen in printed editions is Baudewijn Cabilliau from Ieper in Flanders.

Van Bauhuysen is the author of the line,

Tot tibi sunt dotes, Virgo, quot sidera caelo. (Virgin, your endowments are as numerous as the stars in the sky.)

In a remarkable tour-de-force, Henri du Puy arranged the verse in 1022 different ways, all of which are dactylic hexameters. His versions were published at Antwerp in 1617. Since then mathematicians and versifiers have sought still more possible reworkings of the line. In addition to Latin poetry, Van Bauhuysen also wrote some Flemish songs of a catechetical nature.

Poem 23

Epigrammatum Liber III
*Ad Laurum: Quid animo quietem,
quid amicos pariat*

    Unde pax mihi tanta, Laure, quaeris?
    Unde hoc in pelago tumultuoso,
    Tam molli, placido, favente, laeto,
    Decurrat mea navicella cursu,
5   Nullo turbine, fluctibusque nullis;
    Unde pax mihi tanta, Laure, quaeris?
    Disce, quod didici, lubens docebo.
    Ex quo multa fero, querorque pauca;
    Ex quo pauca loquor, premoque multa;
10 Quaeque nigra videntur, alba credo;
    Quaeque nigra feruntur, alba dico;
    Nec hostes numerare, Laure, possum,
    Nec caros numerare, Laure, possum.

---

4. *yawl:* boat.

Meter: Hendecasyllabic or Phalaecean. The poem is printed on p. 63 of the 1616 Antwerp edition. Book III of the *Epigrams* from which our two selections are taken contained 60 poems.

Title: "What brings peace" to the soul is a neo-Stoic concept to be found frequently in the Jesuit Latin poets. The theme brought to Mertz's mind Shakespeare's *Hamlet* I.3.58: "Give every man thine ear, but few thy voice."

Poem 23

Epigrams Book 3
To Laurus: What brings peace and friends

You ask me, Larry, for the source of my happiness. How, in this stormy sea of life, my little yawl sails along so peacefully smooth and pleasing, with no disturbance from the choppy sea. (5) You ask? I'll gladly let you in on the secret I have learned.

Since I have everything I need, I have few complaints. My speech is brief; I keep my thoughts to myself. What seems black to me I consider white; what people regard as black, I call white. (10) I cannot count any enemies and I can't count any special or more intimate friends.

Text:
8. *querorque pauca:* I make few complaints.
9. *premoque:* And I suppress, And I keep back.

Poem 24

Epigrammatum Liber III
Quis amicus?
Ad Philonem Cordium

    Non nuda vox amicus est, non cassa nux,
    Dilecte Cordi; non, amabilis risus
    Blandique nictus; non ocelli ludii,
    Et dulce flammans frontis aureae lumen;
5   Sint byssina licet verba, Serum vellera,
    Paestique cuncta quae loquare sint flores,
    Sint plena mellis, plena sint amoribus
    Luminaque, et ora, et verba: facta si desint,
    Iam nuda vox amicus est, et cassa nux:
10 Cernitur amicus amore, more, et ore, et re.

Meter: Iambic trimeter, alternating with choliambs (limping iambs or scazons). The poem is published on p. 55 of the 1616 Antwerp edition.

Title: Both *Philo* and *Cordius* suggest love and friendship.

Poem 24

Epigrams Book 3
Who's a Friend?

    The word *friend* is not merely a simple word or an empty sound, dear Heart. It is not merely pleasing laughter; it is not any flattery or blinking or play of the eyes; it is not the golden glow on the face of a smile. Let your words be ever so silky or spun with fleece or the silk of China; (5) let them be like roses from Paestum or honey sweet and expressed with loving affection with the light of the eyes and the glow of the face – if acts are wanting, friendship is an empty sound and empty shell. The real friend is seen in true love, excellent morals, kindness of expression, and good deeds. (10)

Text:

  1. *cassa nux:* an empty nutshell, a trifle. The phrase, although colloquial, is frequent in the poets.

  5. *Serum:* the Chinese, celebrated for their silken fabrics *(vellera)*.

  6. *Paesti:* Ancient Paestum was famous for its twice-blooming roses (*cf.* Virgil, *Georg.* 4.119: *biferique rosaria Paesti*.

  10. The play on words - *amore, more, ore, re* - cannot be expressed in English.

Many Jesuit Latin poets wrote drama

Nicolas Avancini
(1611-1686)

Nicolas Avancini was born at Brez, 51 km. north of Trento, on December 1, 1611. He entered the Society of Jesus on November 14, 1627, while still but 15 years of age. He was a professor of rhetoric and philosophy at Graz for four years and subsequently a professor of theology at Vienna for ten years. He then began his long career as an administrator in the Society of Jesus. He became rector at the colleges of Passau (1664-66), Vienna (1666-69) and Graz (1672-75). In 1672 he became personally known to Roman officials when he was a member of a procurators' congregation in Rome. In 1675 he was appointed Visitor of Bohemia, and then Provincial of the Austrian Province (he served until 1680). In 1682, he was a delegate to the 12th General Congregation and was chosen Assistant for the German Assistancy of the Society of Jesus. He passed away in the Eternal City on December 6, 1686 just six days before the General of the Society, Charles de Noyelle, who had considered appointing Avancini his Vicar General, and thus he would have made Avancini the highest superior of the Jesuits.

Avancini published works on philosophy and theology. He was also the author of sermons, orations, and dramas. His most famous work is *Vita et Doctrina Iesu Christi ex Quattuor Evangelistis Collecta (Life and Doctrine of Jesus Christ Gathered from the Four Gospels)*, a collection of meditations for each day of the year. It has been translated into many European languages. It certainly has been his most lasting work. The poetry of Avancini is of two kinds, lyric and dramatic. The lyric poetry is modeled on Horace and arranged like Horace's in four books of odes and one book of epodes. The collection was published in Vienna in 1659. The dramatic poetry was published at various times as Avancini produced plays for use in the Jesuit colleges. The earliest collection is in three parts, published at Vienna in 1655, 1659, and 1671. Avancini's published plays come to twenty-seven and their themes are usually great historical figures such as Constantine, Theodosius, and Francis Xavier. He certainly is a major figure in Jesuit drama.

Poem 25

Liber III, Ode XXVI
In Morbo

Ad Beatissimam Virginem, Salutem Infirmorum

    Corpus fatiscit, pondus inutile
    Mentique vires denegat. Heu! nimis
        Vires caducae, si cadente
            Corpore, mens quoque collabascit!

5   Heu caeca mens! heu! undique nubilis,
    Densaque tetrae noctis imagine
        Conclusa, in aeternos nitores
            Pigrum animum nequit evibrare!

    In labra lente progrederis, SALUS
10 MARIA morbis; ast animum tamen
        Totum occupasti. Cor amore
            Ardet; at obsequiis amantis

    Vox non secundat. Diligo, diligo
    Te corde toto, VIRGO, Salus mea,
15   Si cogitando mens fatiscit,
            Se reficit cor amore. Qualis

    Madente penna fulminis aliger
    Frustra laborat sese humiles supra
        Librare terras, penneoque
20   Obsequio penetrare nubes;

    Tamen capacem luminis aurei
    Solisque vultum tollit, et aethera
        Visu supergressus negatum
            Spectat iter, superatque vultu:

25 Labante talis corpore, vividum
    Elibro amorem: quodque loqui vetor,
        Sentire fas est. Hoc amantum est,
            Pauca loqui, teneroque corde

    Sentire multa. En Virgo, silentium
30 Pro me perorat. Dum taceo, loquor:
        Amo: nec ultra. Si tacebo
            Plura loquor; quia plus amabo.

Poem 25

Book 3, Ode 26
In Sickness

To the Blessed Virgin
Health of the Sick

I am worn out. My body, useless, is like a heavy weight on my soul. It deprives me of all mental strength. Oh, what failing powers! All about me are clouds filled with specters of dark night. (5) They prevent my soul from seeing the beauties of the eternal. (10) The words, "Mary, Health of the Sick" rise so slowly to my lips, though the heart is warm with love. I love you Lady, I love you, my salvation. Though my mind wearies, my heart restores itself with love. (15) As an eagle with wet wings tries in vain to lift himself from the ground and soar into the clouds, (20) yet keeps his eyes bright and alert, directed to the heights which are beyond his power of flight, (25) so I with failing body, express my love. And what I cannot put in words, I have a right to feel. Lovers have few words, but their hearts beat ardently. (30) The more silent I am, the more I love and shall love.

Meter: Alcaic strophe

Title: Although our selection of Marian poems is limited to this one, poem 12 of Sarbiewski, and poems 39 and 42 in the selections from Balde, the theme is certainly a quite popular one with the Jesuit Latin poets. They all wrote in honor of the Blessed Virgin.

Text:

3. *caducae: caducas* was also read by Mertz and the translation follows that.

4. *collabascit:* "totters at the same time." The word is used only once in Roman authors (Plautus: *Stichus* 4.1.17).

Poem 26

Liber III, Ode XLVII
Ad Annaeum Feronium

Noscere se ipsum summa est scientia.

    Quid Stagyra iuverit
        Exhausta? vel quid Poecilen Zenonis,
    Socratisve pulpita
        Lassasse docta tusse, et abditarum
5   Uberem scientiam
        Bibisse rerum? Si scias recursus
    Siderum vagantium;
        Quo luna fonte cornuum recondat
    Splendidam superbiam,
10   Vel quo sub antro siderum micantes
    Filios puerpera
        Gignat; dies qua luce se capillet
    Quo gradu Venus meet;
        Quot astra caelum censeat; quot aether
15   Ditet influentiis
        Subiecta terrae regna; quo procellae
    Suscitentur Aeoli
        Partu; quis Euripum stato tenore
    Ducat, et resorbeat:

Meter: Hipponactic system. A so-called Euripidean verse (trochaic catalectic dimeter) followed by a catalectic iambic trimeter.

Poem 26

Book 3, Ode 47
To Annaeus Feronius

To know oneself is supreme science.

What if...you studied all of Aristotle's works and all Athenian lore or Socratic thought to the loss of health? What if...you imbibed a knowledge of all abstruse questions? (5) the rotation of the planets? knew where the moon hides the haughty splendor of her horns? where her children, the stars in their beauty, are born? (10) knew where the sun is crowned with light? knew the various phases of Venus, the morning star? What if...you counted all the stars? knew the changes of weather? (16) the source of storms? the rise and fall of tides?

Text:

1. *Stagyra:* This is a place name; so it is used by metonymy for "Aristotle's works." Aristotle was born at Stagira in Chalcidice in 384 B.C.

2. *Poecilen Zenonis:* The *stoa* or portico in Athens that was decorated with paintings by Polygnotus and other artists. Zeno of Citium taught there and his philosophy is called Stoicism.

3. *Socratisve pulpita:* Socrates would deny he had a stage or platform on which to teach. Almost certainly, Avancini, in line with the first two references, alludes to the Platonic school of philosophy.

7. *siderum vagantium:* the planets.

12. *capillet:* this verb does not appear in the active voice in classical Latin but its meaning is clear: provide with hair.

13. *Venus:* Avancini means the planet, not the goddess.

15. *influentiis:* a late Latin word from astrological texts.

17. *Aeoli:* Aeolus was the god of the winds. He ruled the islands between Italy and Sicily where ke kept the winds shut up in caverns.

18. *Euripum:* the channel between Boeotia and Euboea in Greece. Today it is called Egripo. In the humanists' poetry, Euripus is the symbol of the unsteady sea.

20   Si Numen ipsum noveris; tamen te
       Nescias; scies nihil.
          Hoc nos, scientes plurima, imperitos
       Arguit scientiae,
          Quod in reductum proprii theatrum
25   Pectoris sagacius
          Numquam subimus. Quid serat, metatque
       Proximus; quid ebibat
          Petrilla, curiosius notamus.
       Quam cuique foeda sit
30   Turpisque mens, non quaerimus. Feroni, haec
       Maxima est scientia:
          Intrare mentis ultimos recessus,
       Fabulam prius sibi
          Examinandam sistere in theatro
35   Mentis, antequam Deo
          Libranda detur. Omnium recenset
       Et probat, vel improbat
          Momenta Iudex. Nemo displicere
       Cum velit Deo, decet
40   Sic ordinare fabulam, ut probetur.

Text:

20-21. A Latin paraphrase of the Greek *gnothi seauton:* words attributed to Chilo, the Lacedaemonian, and to Solon, the Athenian. It was inscribed in gold on the facade of Apollo's temple at Delphi.

33-34. *fabulam examinandam:* cf. Shakespeare, *As You Like It* II.7.139: "All the world's a stage".

38. *Iudex:* the 1659 Vienna edition reads *Index* (p. 299), but clearly that is an error for *Iudex*. Mertz translated *Index*. The *u* of *Iudex* was printed upside down.

What if...you had a knowledge of the very deity itself? (20) But did not know yourself? You would know nothing. The fact is we never enter into the theater of our own heart. In idle curiosity we know what our neighbor sows and what he reaps; what secret thoughts are in the mind we never question. Real knowledge, my dear Feronius, is to enter the secret recesses of the heart and stage the play of our own life before it is put on in God's presence. The great Witness will prove or disprove all points. No one, if he thinks of hurting God's feelings, will play to receive plaudits.

Malapert defends Coster in Poem 27

Charles Malapert
(1581-1631)

Charles Malapert, one of the earliest Jesuit poets and mathematicians, was born at Mons, Hainault, now in southwestern Belgium, June 12, 1581. He entered the Society of Jesus on November 17, 1600. A zealous apostle, Malapert studied and taught philosophy in Lorraine, mathematics in Poland and at Douai, and was rector at the college of Arras from 1627 to 1630. He was answering a request of Philip IV to begin a course of mathematics at Madrid when he died on his way there at Victoria, Catalonia, on November 5, 1631.

Malapert's published work includes not only poetry, but also treatises and addresses on mathematics and astronomy. The collection of poems, which begins with a dedication to Prince Ladislaus of Poland, was published at Antwerp in 1616 with Bernard Van Bauhuysen's poetry. The poetry consists of a tragedy in five acts entitled *Sedecias*. Two books in hexameters discuss the winds *(De Ventis, On the Winds)*. There are nine elegiac poems that treat of Christ's passion, beginning with the Last Supper *(Christus Patiens, The Suffering Christ)*. Finally, there is a collection of 23 poems, dedicated to Louis XIII, King of France and Navarre, with the title *Miscellaneorum liber I*.

Malapert enjoyed a high reputation among his contemporaries for his Latinity and good taste. Certainly his mathematical works and poems show a man of versatility and talent. At times he indulges in sarcasm and bitter invective, but these were commonplace in the religious controversies of the time.

Poem 27

Miscellaneorum Liber:
Pro insulo anagrammatismo:
Franciscus Costerus Iesuita
"CERTO TU ES ASINUS AFRICUS – SIC"
Auctori Reponitur:
Lucas Osiander Praedicantius
"NIL TU ASINE CARPES, I AD CARDUOS"

    Cervice torta, mille carnifex modis
    Fingis, refingis cereum nomen mihi,
    Asinumque, miro grammatum textu facis.
    Numquam futurum ni tuum SIC adsuas;
5   Sic inficetum! sic inurbanum! quasi
    Suam tibi addat uxor in cristas colum.
    Vis me Africano genere prognatum; papae!
    Longe id petitum est, omniumque ingratius:
    Nam quis asinorum Punicum celebrat genus?
10 Unicum Apuleius Afer Africum canit
    Aureus Asellum; subole sed nulla ferunt
    Usquam beatum, Iuppiter, factum male.
    Tibi vero stemma sanguine Arcadico inclytum,
    Ante et Gigantum proelia, et lunae globum
15 Caelo micantem: genere mortali altior,
    Stirpe invidenda tangis antiquum chaos.
    Nisi fallor, haesit nomen hinc Graecum tibi,
    Fertile elementis, quae tuam gentem arguant;
    Sive tu Osiander, sive Onander diceris,
20 Hoc tute genere macte sis, per me licet.

Meter: Iambic senarius

Title: Malapert did not number the 23 poems that make up the *Miscellaneorum liber.* This poem is printed on pp. 111-12 of the 1616 Antwerp edition.

    Charles Malapert's Rector, Francis Coster, S.J. had been insulted by Lucas Osiander, one of Martin Luther's followers, in an insipid anagram. Malapert answered the insult in an anagram on the preacher's name. The letters in the two men's names are rearranged to spell out the verses. Osiander's anagram reads:
        You certainly are an African ass; (*sic!* that's sure.)
Malapert's answer reads:
        You jackass, you can't graze here; go back to your thistles.
Anagrams were immensely popular in the seventeenth century; there are hundreds of them.

    Coster himself had written a pamphlet in 1604 to answer Osiander. He complained in the dedicatory letter that the eight theses that Osiander was attacking had been published twenty years before and were objectionable to Calvinists, but not to Lutherans.

    The translation was made by John E. Festle, S.J. (1925-83).

Poem 27

Miscellaneous Poems:
The author of this tasteless anagram
Francis Coster, Jesuit
"YOU CERTAINLY ARE AN AFRICAN ASS – THAT'S SURE"
is answered as follows:
Lucas Osiander, Preacher
"YOU JACKASS, YOU CAN'T GRAZE HERE;
GO BACK TO YOUR THISTLES"

Like the utter blunderer you are, you bend over backwards working and reworking my name like wax. You juggle the letters amazingly and end up with ASS. The effort falls flat unless you add on SIC. Ah, that infelicitous, that crude SIC, (5) like your spouse hitching a distaff to her hairdo. You make me a scion of Afric blood. Ugh! Pretty far-fetched, and the really insulting touch. Who sings the praises of Punic asses? (10) Only the golden African, Apuleius writes of a poor little African ass; but, heavens, they say the ill-constructed thing was never blessed with offspring.

For yourself, you claim a noble descent to origins Arcadian, antedating even the battles of the Giants and the day the moon in the sky lit up the world. Yes, you are more than an ordinary man. (15) Your enviable line harks back to the prehistoric chaos. I may be wrong, but this is why your name is Greek and teems with primitive elements that betray your species. I don't care whether you call yourself Holy Joe or simply Assy Jack. The family's a well-established one, and I congratulate you on it. (20).

Text:

1. *carnifex:* As a term of reproach, it means "scoundrel, villain, rascal".

5. *inficetum:* alternate of *infacetum,* "coarse, blunt, rude".

6. *cristas:* This is the reading in the 1616 Antwerp edition. The final *s* is very faint and was unduly omitted in the 1634 Antwerp edition.

10. *Apuleius:* Lucius Apuleius (b.c. 123 A.D.) was from Madaura in Africa. Malapert refers to Apuleius' novel *Metamorphoses,* or as it is commonly called, *The Golden Ass.* Malapert transfers the epithet "Golden" to Apuleius himself.

13. *Arcadico:* Varro (*R.R.* 2.1.14) and others tell us that the Arcadian ass was valued for stud purposes. Malapert jokes that there is no known offspring of Apuleius' Golden Ass.

19. *Onander:* Malapert seems to be distorting Osiander's name to bring it closer to the Greek words *onos* and *aner* (ass-man). *Onager* is the word for wild ass, but does not enter in here.

20. *dedolatus:* cudgelled soundly, thoroughly thrashed.

Sed te impudenter ut sacris sic ingeras
Animal profanum, ruminare nescium,
Nec ungue fisso, moneo, per me non licet;
Nec lege liceat. Abstine ergo, si sapis,
25   Dentem ungulamque, scriptionibus sacris:
Nam licet hianti saepe rictu prensites,
Nil asine carpes, ad tuos i carduos
Aut fuste referes dedolatus hinc pedem.

What I won't stand is this: it's unnatural for a pagan beast like yourself, incapable of chewing a cud, not even cloven-footed, to meddle *sic* in things sacred. I warn you not to! If you know what's good for you, leave off dancing and dining on Holy Writ. (25) Your wide-open trap may occasionally snap, but, Jackass, you'll get nothing. Off to your thistles or you'll return home with a sound thrashing.

Poem 28

Miscellaneorum Liber:
In calumniatorem

Ridere amici vultis? ecce fabellam.
Scotus Lovani nuper excucullatus,
Nimiumque mollis Ordinis sacri tyro,
In sacra demens pessimos facit versus.
5   Scotus ille iamiam qui pedem extullit ludo,
Aurem magistris vellit, has agit grates.
Ille, ille, nostro transfuga laris incerti
Tecto receptus, qui domesticum in panem
Toties caninos strinxit impiger dentes,
10 Nostrum canino dente lancinat nomen
Dentire cum vix coeperit poetaster,
Censete, amici, num bonum sit factum
Aures ut altum promicent cucullato,
Tergum ut superbo pruriat magistello,
15 Dentesque longe dentiant poetastro.

Meter: Choliambs or scazons
Title: The unnumbered poem's text is printed on pp. 114-15 of the 1616 Antwerp edition.

Poem 28

Miscellaneous Poems:
The Pettifogger

Is it a laugh you want? Here's a story.

Recently a Scot, novice of a religious order, altogether too immature, was defrocked at Louvain. The fool wrote some very insulting verses against a religious rite. The fellow, trying his first step in this type game, (5) nipped the ears of his teacher. This was his act of gratitude. The poor fellow, out on his own and without a home, was taken into one of our houses. He was quick to show his teeth, which he often bared at our table. The pettifogger with a dog's snap tears our good name to pieces, (10) although he had scarcely begun to cut his teeth.

Friends, you judge for yourselves whether it isn't right that his ears stand high above his cowl, that even a second-rate teacher itches to give him a thrashing. It will take a long time for him to cut his teeth on this poetizing. (15)

Text:

2. *Lovani:* at Louvain.

2. *excucullatus:* defrocked. Although Silver Age Latin authors knew of a kind of head-covering called a *cucullus,* in medieval Latin, the word was transferred to the frock. I find no attestation of the verb form Malapert uses here.

3. *sacri:* This is clearly the reading in the 1616 Antwerp edition, and can be explained as a "minor order" or, perhaps, even as "tonsure". The alternative reading *sancti* does not scan.

11. *dentire:* to cut teeth, to teethe.

14. *pruriat:* "he itches for a beating."

14. *magistello:* I find no attestation of this diminutive. Mertz has opted to take the pejorative sense of the diminutive, "second-rate" teacher. It could also have been rendered "poor, insulted teacher". Professor IJsewijn notes that John Clarke, headmaster of Lincoln School, uses *magistellulus* in his *Querela Apologetica* (1632). See *Humanistica Lovaniensia* 25 (1976), p. 270.

Master of Elegy

Sidronius De Hossche
(1596-1653)

Sidronius De Hossche (Sidronius Hosschius) was born on January 20, 1596 at Merkem in western Flanders. His father was a shepherd on the estate of an ancient Benedictine abbey, which had become the property of the Jesuits. The son took care of the sheep and, when old enough, started his studies with the Jesuits at Ieper.

De Hossche entered the Society of Jesus on October 20, 1616 at Ieper. One of his fellow novices was John Berchmans, the future canonized saint. De Hossche's health was so poor that officials of the Society considered dismissing him. He begged to be allowed to stay, even if he had to change his status and become a brother. In 1620 for his regency, De Hossche was sent to the college of Hertogenbosch as teacher of fourth year Latin and poetry. Here he also later served as principal for over 800 students, many of whom came from Holland and other Protestant districts. In 1629 the town surrendered to the forces of the United Provinces, after a five-month siege, and the bishop and priests were given the choice of giving up their city or their faith. They did not wait the two months granted, but made a quick decision and picked up bag and baggage, and after leaving four Fathers to care for the Catholics, left on carts and on foot for Antwerp.

At Antwerp, De Hossche was again appointed principal and he remained there from 1632 to 1634. Fr. Willem De Wael, provincial, then changed the whole tenor of De Hossche's life. For Fr. De Wael assigned De Hossche to teach Jesuit scholastics in the humanities and classics. He did so for 13 years with great success. To show his gratitude, De Hossche wrote a 90 line elegy to De Wael, which concludes with the following elegiac couplets:

> Vicimus, O Musae! venientem admittite vatem;
>   Guilielmus votis annuit ecce meis.
> Hic favet, hoc satis est. Populi vesana valete
>   Murmura: Guilielmo Iudice tutus ero (*Elegies* 2.6).

We have prevailed, O Muses! Give admittance to the coming poet;
behold William has nodded approval to my prayers.
He favors, this is enough. Farewell to crazy murmurs
of the mob: with William as judge I will be safe.

Those thirteen years (1637-1649) were spent at Kortrijk, which finally fell to the French. The next two years De Hossche taught at the court of the Hapsburg prince, Archduke Leopold William of Austria, Governor of the Spanish Netherlands, but life at court did not suit this simple shepherd's son, and he turned to preaching. On January 29, 1652, he was appointed superior of the Jesuit community at Tongeren, where he died the following year at the age of fifty-seven.

De Hossche's poetic works were first printed as occasional pieces upon such events as the publication of some theological treatises by Leonard Lessius, or as an act of thanksgiving to the Blessed Virgin, written for the chapel of the Jesuit house of Kortrijk, and congratulatory poems to Leopold William. The scattered pieces were first gathered by Jacob Vande Walle in 1656, three years after De Hossche's death. The title of Vande Walle's collection is *Sidronii Hosschii e Societate Iesu Elegiarum Libri Sex (Sidronius De Hossche's Six Books of Elegies)*, but that title is a bit misleading, for the collection was never designed to be put together in six books. Indeed, the 1656 edition does not use the enumeration of Books IV to VI at all. Rather, the breakdown of De Hossche's poems in that edition is as follows: Bk. I: *Cursus Vitae Humanae (Course of Human Life)*, nine elegies, all of which use sea and ship imagery; Bk. II: No title, 18 occasional pieces, his expression of gratitude to Willem De Wael being the sixth; Bk. III: No title, 12 elegies, then two hexameters on *Epistolae heroicae (Letters of Heroes)* and the *Silva (Miscellany);* unnumbered Book IV (book I of the second cycle): *Christus Patiens (Suffering Christ)*. These elegiac poems were the first major publication of De Hossche and attracted the attention of Leopold William, who asked De Hossche to teach first his pages, and then his own two sons. De Hossche spent two years in that teaching position. There follows: unnumbered Bk V. (book II of the second cycle): *Lacrimae Sancti Petri (The Tears of St. Peter)*, 11 poems on the repentance and sorrow of Peter after his denial of Christ. Finally there is unnumbered Bk. VI (book III of the second cycle). This sixth book contains elegiac poems on current events.

Much of De Hossche's poetry is of a very personal kind. The poems give glimpses of his interior life as he contemplates the passion of Christ, the penitence of Peter, or the sorrows of Mary under the cross. His warmth is shown in the pieces addressed to Willem De Wael, Sarbiewski, and other contemporary Jesuits. He was a master of form, and while he might not deserve the high praises that some have lavished upon him, yet he remains one of the greatest of the Jesuit Latin poets. The citizens of Merkem erected a monument to him in the village square in the nineteenth century.

Poem 29

Liber II, Elegia XVIII
Ad Somnum

    Somne, quies animi, curarum, Somne, levamen,
        Et primus placidos inter habende Deos:
    Seu prope Cimmerios tua te tenet aula iacentem,
        Seu legis in tenera molle papaver humo:
5   Seu geminas aperis valvas, habituraque mittis
        Somnia, seu mittis non habitura fidem.
    Huc ades, et tacitis allabens leniter alis,
        Nostra soporifera lumina tange manu.
    Decubui: sed enim multo iam tempore noctis
10   Sum vigil, et lasso corpore: Somne, veni!

          • • •

    Nec canis ad limen, nec sub trabe garrula Progne,
        Garrula iam Progne, iam tacuere canes.
    Nunc etiam nox alta favet, nunc humidus aër,
20   Lunaque somniferis humida rorat aquis.
    Vincinis tantum foliis immurmurat aura,
        Et rivus tremulae lene susurrat aquae.
    Somne, veni; cristata cadet tibi caesa volucris,
        Spargentur pennae lacte meroque tuae.

          • • •

25   Ipse seram tenerum placita tibi nocte papaver
        Unde tuis nectam serta gerenda comis.
    Ipse tibi laudes, votivaque carmina solvam,
        Tu modo ne desis laudibus ipse tuis.
    Tu reparas vires, reddisque laboribus aptas,

Meter: Elegiac distich. Selections of the 96 lines of text have been chosen and translated.

Poem 29

Book 2, Elegy 18:
To Sleep

Sleep, gentle sleep, rest to heart and solace care,
    First of the gods to be invoked,
Whether you abide in far off northern halls
    Or find your comfort in the poppy fields,
5 Or open up the twin gates of ivory or of horn,
    True for one and doubtful of the other —
Do come and with gentle wings fan lightly
    My tired eyes which long for sleep.
I have reclined, but for so long a period of the night
10   I'm wide awake and wearied in the flesh.

• • •

The night is far advanced, no dog barks at the gate,
    No swallow keeps chattering at the eaves.
The morning dew is settling on the field bathed in moonlight,
20   The leaves are murmuring in the nearby copse,
The brook is babbling silently in its bed.
    Dear sleep, do come. The morning cock has made his call;
Let feathers fall with taste of milk and sweet wine,
    Peacefully soft whispering sleep.

• • •

25 I'll weave from poppy a garland for the night
    To decorate your hair with garland green;
I'll sing your praises with a votive song,
    If you stand true to promises made.
You restore new strength for labors fit,

Text:

3. *Cimmerios:* A fabulous people thought to dwell in caves between Baiae and Cumae. Since perpetual darkness prevailed among them, there Somnus made his dwelling. See Ovid, *Meta.* 11.592.

17. *Progne:* Procne, who was changed into a swallow.

20. *rorat:* bedews.

23-24. Sacrifices will be made to Sleep. Mertz's translation fails to bring out the idea of sacrifice.

30   Tu sistis lacrimas, aegraque corda levas.
        Quod neque divitiae possunt conferre, nec aurum,
          Quod nec honor titulis omnibus, ipse potes.
        Tu curas circum regalia sceptra volantes,
          Et procul invisos cogis abesse metus.

          • • •

55   Nil ago! blanditias, et non tibi debita verba
          Perdimus, O tenebris turpior ipse tuis.
        Somne niger, nigro cui pectus concolor ori;
          Ferree, nec mites inter habende Deos.
        Noxia, Somne, quies, iacturaque maxima vitae:
60   Haec, haec sunt meritis nomina digna tuis.

          • • •

65   Eumenidum frater, metuendaque mortis imago,
          Sis procul, et longe lumina nostra fuge.

Text:
65. *Eumenidum:* euphemistic name for the Furies.

30   You stop all tears, and ease the heart of grief;
       No wealth, no gold, no honored titles are of avail
         What you can do in gentle soothing way.
       You scatter far the worries of the royal crown,
         And bid all fears depart from your domain.

● ● ●

55   No words avail! and flattery will not help.
       We waste our time! O cruel sleep,
     More dark than your own native darkness.
       Your heart is dark, so iron cold
     No title of the godhead yours, a loss of life
60   The only titles yours in truth.

● ● ●

65   Brother of the Fiends, true image of death,
       Stay far from me, flee from my tired eyes.

SIDRONII HOSSCHII VITA;

Ex Bibliotheca Scriptorum Societatis Jesu.

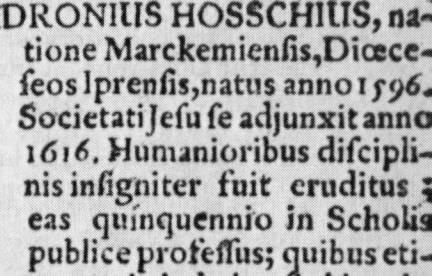

IDRONIUS HOSSCHIUS, natione Marckemienfis, Dioeceseos Iprenfis, natus anno 1596. Societati Jefu fe adjunxit anno 1616. Humanioribus difciplinis infigniter fuit eruditus; eas quinquennio in Scholis publice profeffus; quibus etiam juniores noftros 13. annis imbuit, & biennio Ephebos Sereniffimi Archiducis LEOPOLDI GUILIELMI tunc Belgii Gubernatoris, Conciones infuper habitæ annos aliquot. Vir profundiffimæ demiffionis & contemptus fui, humile & paftoritium genus quo ortus fuit, jucundè folebat domi forisque commemorare, non fecùs ac familiæ fuæ decora & ftirpis fplendorem. In tyrocinio cum perpetuo corporis languore afflictaretur, videreturque non fatis aptus ad Societatis munia, adeoque ad fuos remittendus, fummoperè contendit, ut in domefticorum adjutorum ordinem potiùs adfcriberetur, quàm à Societate amandaretur. Retentus itáque eft magno fuo ac Societatis bono. Moderatoribus fuis femper ad nutum fuit obfequentiffimus, & ad quosvis labores diurnos juxta ac nocturnos promptus ac impiger. In obeundis pietatis exercitationibus

Poem 30 is addressed to Sidronius De Hossche

Jacob Vande Walle
(1599-1690)

Jacob Vande Walle (Wallius) was born at Kortrijk on September 14, 1599. He entered the Society of Jesus on October 19, 1617. His apostolates included the teaching of humanities and rhetoric, serving as prefect of studies, and being a mission-giver and preacher. Vande Walle died at Antwerp on March 9, 1690, having been a Jesuit for 73 years and a priest for 63.

As for most of the Jesuit Latin poets, so for Vande Walle, many of the pieces appeared separately for some special occasion. For example, Vande Walle's poem in honor of Sarbiewski appears in a 1632 edition of that poet. As we saw above, Vande Walle was responsible for the first complete collection of De Hossche's poems. On that occasion Vande Walle wrote a memorial poem for his deceased fellow Jesuit and poet. However, the main collection of Vande Walle's poetry was published at Antwerp in 1656 under the title *Iacobi Wallii e Scoietate Iesu Poematum libri IX* (Jacob Vande Walle, S.J.'s *Nine Books of Poems*). Books I and II are called *Heroica,* not so much because they have epic themes, but because they are written in dactylic hexameters. Book III is made up of a number of paraphrases of Horace's poems. The meter is once again dactylic hexameter and the treatment is far more expansive than Horace's. Books IV-VI are elegies. The third of these elegy books (the sixth in the entire collection) is entitled *Oliva Pacis (Olive Branch of Peace)* and consists of six poems, all of which call for peace. Books VII-IX are lyric poems. The first four poems are on Jesuit saints. Others are addressed to De Hossche (our selection) and Sarbiewski.

Vande Walle has a clear, pure Latin style. He showed versatility in the many genres he attempted.

Poem 30

Liber I, Ode X

Ad Sidronium Hosschium e Societate Iesu
Cum ab eo cultissimam accepisset elegiam

      O gratos mihi, gratiisque plenos,
      O cultos elegos, et expolitos,
      Quos ad Pegaseae caput scatebrae
      Dictarunt faciles tibi Camenae!
5   Nusquam simplicitas, decensque cultus,
      Et nusquam nitor, eruditioque,
      Et nusquam veneres, salesque desunt.
      O cultos elegos, et expolitos,
      O gratos mihi, gratiisque plenos!
10   An spectem numeros? tenentur aures.
      An cultum? capior. modosne? ducor.
      Sensus? robur habent. tuamne limam?
      Nil exactius est, politiusque.
      Artem? summa latet. measne laudes?
15   Hoc tantum (sed amoris ista culpa est,
      Et gratae venia est parata culpae)
      Peccarunt elegi, tuaeque Musae.

Meter: Hendecasyllabic or Phalaecean

Poem 30

Book 1, Ode 10
To Sidronius De Hossche of the Society of Jesus when he received from him a most courteous poem

What a joy to receive your grateful elegies, so cultured, so polished – elegies the Muses, your friends, dictated under the influence of prancing Pegasus. Nowhere is there clearer diction and reverence, (5) and nowhere more refinement and learning. No charm or wit is lacking. If I listen to the meter, my ears are captivated by the harmony; (10) if I look for eloquence, I am overwhelmed; if it is balance of lines and feeling and polish, nothing is more exact, nothing more delicate and refined. And what artistic concept! where art disappears when art is used. And my praise! but here is the fault (15) and I cry for mercy in my faulty interpretation. The fault is in your elegies and your Muses!

Text:

3. *Pegasea:* pertaining to Pegasus, the winged horse of the Muses. A blow from Pegasus' hoof made Hippocrene, the fountain of the Muses, to spring up on Mt. Helicon.

4. *Camenae:* the Muses.

12. *limam:* Since Horace's *labor limae* (*Ars Poet.* 291), the file *(lima)* is essential equipment for the poet.

15-17. The correct sense is: Praise of Vande Walle is the only fault in De Hossche's elegies, but that defect is assigned to love and easily forgiven.

Jacobus Balde Vates Boiorum

The Horace of Germany

Jacob Balde
(1604-1668)

Jacob Balde, the Horace of Germany, nine years younger than Matthias Casimir Sarbiewski, the Horace of Poland, was born around January 4, 1604 in the free town of Ensisheim in Upper Alsace. He was the second oldest boy in a family of three girls and five boys, one other of whom also became a Jesuit. Early in life Balde was sent to Belfort to acquire a thorough knowledge of French, a necessary language for the legal profession chosen for him by his father. Later he studied the classics and rhetoric in the Jesuit colleges at Molsheim and in his native town. In 1621, he left Alsace for Ingolstadt in Bavaria when peace was disturbed by the Thirty Years' War. He was never to revisit his native land.

At Ingolstadt he studied philosophy and law. This was to occasion a complete change in his life. Because of his wit and ability to improvise song, he became a favorite companion of the students on their visits to local taverns. In one of his frolics, he played the mandolin and serenaded a miller's daughter. She did not take to his madrigal and closed the shutters of the window and left Balde down in the mouth. Then he heard monks singing early matins at a nearby religious house, and true to his character, he smashed the mandolin against the wall with the words, *"Cantatum satis est; frangito barbiton"* "That is the end of the song; let the mandolin be broken".

The next day he asked permission from the Jesuit provincial to become a Jesuit. In due time Balde received the major superior's *"placet"* or permission to enter and on July 1, 1624 he entered the novitiate at Landsberg. Upon the conclusion of two years of novitiate, Balde did his regency at Munich and Innsbruck (1626-30). He studied theology at Ingolstadt (1630-34), and was ordained to the priesthood on September 24, 1633. His first teaching assignments as a priest were at Ingolstadt (1635-37) and

Munich (1637-50), at which latter place Balde also served as sodality director, as court preacher, and, though unsuccessful at it, as court historian. He soon acquired a wide reputation as an outstanding scholar and teacher. Some contemporaries called him a Second Quintilian. From 1650 to 1653, Balde was at Landshut and Amberg, where his chief apostolate was preaching. Due to failing health he was sent to Neuburg on the Danube in 1654 where he became the favorite of the young Jesuit students and the intimate friend and adviser of Count Palatine Philip Wilhelm. He died at Neuburg on August 9, 1668.

Balde's numerous poetical works, written mostly in Latin, were marked by a brilliant imagination, nobility of thought, tender affection, wit and humor, knowledge of the human heart, and profound learning. He had a remarkable grasp of standard Latin authors from Plautus to Claudian and always employed true classical Latin diction. His poems and other writings deal in their range with the ideas of the world in which he lived: religion, love of friends, love of country, arts and letters, the virtues of patient endurance and fortitude. Over seventy odes honor the Blessed Virgin Mary. His patriotic poems, according to Herder, make him a German poet for all times.

Balde was a master of classical Latin, wielding it with power and originality in verse structure, poetic form, and diction. Like Horace (and Sarbiewski), Balde wrote four books of odes and one of epodes. In imitation of Statius, he wrote nine books of *Silva Lyrica (A Medley of Lyric Poems)*. Balde tried his hand at epic verse in such poems as the *Batrachomyomachia (The Battle of the Frogs and Mice)* in five books and the *De vanitate mundi (On the Vanity of the World)*. Among his satirical poems are found twenty-two poems on the *Gloria medicinae (The Glory of Medicine)* and one *Contra abusum tabaci (Against the Abuse of Tobacco)*. Balde also wrote dramatic poetry, the most important of which is the *Iepthtias (The Daughter of Jephthah),* first performed by the students at Ingolstadt in 1637 and at many other Jesuit schools thereafter. Balde wrote the music as well for this colossal piece, which took seven hours in the performing. The text of the play, however, was not published until 1654. Balde's biographers with no little justification admire him as one of the most versatile poets who ever wrote.

Poem 31

Liber I, Ode III
Thomae Mori constantia

Hic ille Morus, quo melius nihil
Titan Britanno vidit ab aethere.
   Funesta cum regem Bolena
      Illicito furiasset aestu,

5   Audax iniquas spernere nuptias
Amore veri propositum minis
   Obvertit Henrici tyranno
      Fortior indocilisque flecti.

Non carcer illum, non Aloysia
10   Dimovit uxor, nec trepidus gener,
   Nec ante patrem Margarita
      Femineo lacrimosa questu.

Fertur monentem mitia coniugem,
Sed non et isto digna viro, procul
15   Abs se remotam cum feroci
      Ut fatuam pepulisse risu.

Mox, qua fluentem se Thamesis rotat,
Ad destinatum funeribus locum
   Casto coronandus triumpho
20   Per medios properavit Anglos.

Meter: Alcaic strophe

Title: Mertz also used the title "The Knight of Constancy". The translation of this poem is one of the few that have been published. Mertz published his version of Book I, Ode 3 in *The Catholic Lawyer* VI.3 (Summer, 1960) p. 258-59. As a tribute to Fr. Mertz, G. Marc'hadour, the editor, reprinted the poem, Mertz's translation, and a German version in *Moreana* XXIII.90 (June, 1986), p. 89-92.

   The poem may have been composed to honor the first centenary of More's death. Verses 10-28 imitate and sometimes verbally echo Horace's description of Regulus, Rome's martyr at Carthage (*Carm.* 3.5.41-52).

Poem 31

Book 1, Ode 3

The Constancy of Thomas More

This is that famous Thomas More; no grander sight
    The sun beheld in England's farflung reign,
When Boleyn, deadly in her guile, drove mad
    The king, unhallowed through Love's wild domain.

5   Strong in his love of truth, More boldly spurned
    The sinful marriage, daring to meet the threat
Of Henry; stronger than the tyrant king,
    Unswayed and resolute, in his purpose set.

No prison keep, no wife could turn his mind;
10   No son-in-law, alarmed with timid fears,
Could make him swerve - no, not his daughter Meg
    Before her father pleading with her tears.

His wife, Dame Alice, spoke of milder ways –
    A course not worthy of the hero's race;
15   He brushed aside her senseless, fatuous plea,
    A smile of sadness playing on his face.

Soon where the Thames its swirling waters poured
    Along the station destined for his death,
In humble triumph to receive the crown
20   He hastened on through folk with bated breath.

Text:

1. *Morus:* Sir Thomas More, Lord Chancellor of England and humanist, born February 7, 1477 and executed for high treason at London, July 6, 1535.

2. *Titan:* a grandson of the first Titan, son of Hyperion, a sun-god.

3. *Bolena:* Anne Boleyn (1507-1536), second wife of Henry VIII. She was condemned to death the year after More.

9. *carcer:* the London Tower.

9. *Aloysia:* Alice Middleton, More's second wife whom he married in 1510.

10. *trepidus gener:* William Roper, More's son-in-law, who was also More's first biographer.

11. *Margarita:* Margaret Roper, More's oldest and favorite daughter whom he called Meg.

Ductum secuta flente Britannia
Non flevit unus marmore durior
   Et certa despectante vultu
      Fata tuens hilarisque torvum.

25 Atqui sciebat, quid sibi regius
Tortor parasset; non aliter tamen
   Quam laureatos Sulla fasces,
      Ipse suam petiit securim.

Plenus futuri quo tumulo stetit,
30 Postquam paventem carnificis manum
   Mercede firmasset, cruento
      Colla dedit ferienda ferro.

Text:

23-24. An earlier version of these lines was: A light of joy brightened his face alone/Grim was his smile, his heart on God alone.

24. *torvum:* adverb here, "fiercely, grimly, gloomily".

27. *Sulla:* In 88 B.C., Sulla marched on Rome to reclaim the command against Mithridates.

29. *tumulo:* Tower Hill.

32. An earlier version of the line was: Of bloody ax, in God's good service bold.

They led him on and though kind England wept,
    His eyes were dry; more firm than quarried stone
He stood and faced the fixed decree of fate;
    Grimly he smiled, his heart on God alone,
25   Though well he knew what tyranny devised
    In way of torture; once Roman Sulla sought
The honored fasces - More with greater love
    Longed for the ax which loyalty had brought.

On Tower Hill with eyes on heaven fixed
30   He calmed the executioner's hand with gold,
He bowed his head to fall beneath the blow
    Of bloody ax, in knighthood's service old.

Poem 32

Liber I, Ode XI
Commendat Flavii Leonis vinum.

Vinum Falerno nectare dulcius
Et quale nunquam protulerit Rhodos,
   Assuesce crystallum subire
      Lene fluens phialaque fundi.

5 Velis solutum compede dolii
Mensam Leonis visere crebrius,
   Hoc Castor et Pollux amici,
      Hoc avidi Lupiceius orat

Comes Melichi; tu neque nubila
10 Fundo minaris, nec capiti graves
   Inducis umbras, nec feroci
      Bella geris metuenda thyrso.

Sed mite duci prolicis hospitem
Quamvis paventem; te penes et ioci
15   Castaeque Musarum camenae
      Et teneri sine lite risus.

Te Iuno furtim, forsan et inscia
Iunone laetus Iuppiter hauserit;
   Malitque Bacchus se relicto
20   Te bibere et suus hinc renasci.

Meter: Alcaic strophe

Title: Mertz's translation suggests a poem on wine in general; Balde, however, praises Flavius Leo's wine in particular.

Poem 32

Book 1, Ode 11
In Praise of Wine to Flavius Leo

O wine, more sweet than Rhodian
    Or e'en Falernian yellow,
Come fill my glass and let me drink
    Your nectar soft and mellow.

5   Be often drawn from cellar cask
    To grace the table festive,
For here like Helen's brothers all
    We're friends with food digestive.

No cloud e'er comes from your bouquet,
10   To dull the drinker's thinking;
Within your cups no wrangling lurks
    To harsher actions sinking.

Mine host may fear the longer draughts
    Which subtly you're inviting;
15   You're full of lightly bantering jests
    And songs with laughter lighting.

Perhaps e'en Juno took a drop,
    And Jove, his dame unknowing,
And Bacchus, too, would gladly be
20   Reborn to taste your glowing.

Text:

1. *Falerno nectare:* Falernian wine. The *Falernus ager* was in Campania at the foot of Mt. Massicus. It was famous in antiquity for its wines.

2. *Rhodos:* Virgil (*Georg.* 2.102) praises the Rhodian grape as *dis et mensis accepta secundis,* "accepted by the gods and for desserts". The island of Rhodes produced a fine wine, but not as good as Flavius Leo's.

7-9. Although Mertz made the identification of Castor and Pollux with Helen's brothers, the four individuals named in these verses seem to be fictional. The latter two certainly are.

10. *fundo:* from the *bottom* of the cup when it is emptied.

13. *prolicis:* from *prolicio, prolicere,* to entice.

15. *camenae:* as a common noun by metonymy: "songs".

Poem 33

Liber I, Ode XII
Ad amphoram cerevisiariam

O nata Capri sidere frigido,
Seu tu querelam sive geris minas,
   Seu ventris insanum tumultum et
      Difficilem, mala testa, somnum;

5 Quocumque servas nomine toxicum,
Numquam moveri digna bono die,
   Averte nolenti poetae
      Promere languidius venenum.

Non ille, quamquam Gorgoneis madet
10 Assuetus undis, te bibet horridus.
   Narratur et Boius Menalcas
      Saepe tuo doluisse aceto.

Tu triste tormentum ingenio admoves
Plerumque leni; tu sapientium
15   Et pectus oblimas et ora,
      Ne retegant animum fidelem.

Te pestilentem neglegit anxius
Dives; sed addis cornua pauperi
   Post te neque iratos trementi
20   Regum apices neque militum arma.

Te messor et, quae cocta aderit, Ceres
Segnesque nodum solvere rustici
   Unctaeque producent lucernae,
      Dum rediens fugat astra Phoebus.

Meter: Alcaic strophe

Title: Balde writes a parody of Horace *Carm.* 3.21. Echoes and exact verbal repetitions of Horace abound in every stanza of the poem.

Poem 33

Book 1, Ode 12
The Stein of Beer

    The stein of beer from butt in cellar cold,
        Full oft the cause of quarrels and bitter tears,
    How many stomach-aches your guzzlings hold,
        How many sleepless nights beset with fears.

5   No matter by what name they call your brew,
        As lager beer unworthy of display;
    Stay far from me, a poet unwilling, who
        Would drink the subtle poison you betray,

    Not he, though steeped in Gorgon's blood, will long
10   Drink of your brew; full oft the story's told
    How French Menalcas, shepherd, tough and strong
        In pain was doubled by your acid cold.

    You sadly give release in pleasant way,
        You cloud the brain and workings of the wise,
15   And on the face of man you will betray,
        The deeper moods of fancy he'd disguise.

    The worried rich man spurns you, sorry stein,
        But you give courage to the poor man's heart;
    When he has drunk him full no kingly line
20   Nor armed soldiery will make him start.

    The reaper and his stein of Ceres brewed,
        The farmer, slow to act, in drinking zest,
    Will drink throughout the night and feel renewed
        When morning sun will put the stars to rest.

Text:

1. *Capri:* "the Goat", a star in the left shoulder of the constellation Auriga (Wagoner).

4. *mala testa:* "wicked jug".

9-10. *Gorgoneis...undis:* "Gorgons' waves". This may allude to the fact that from the blood of the Gorgon Medusa, Pegasus sprang. Pegasus in turn struck the ground with his hoof and thus caused the spring of Hippocrene to flow. Or the allusion may be to the snakes in the Gorgons' hair or around their waists. The latter is more likely.

11. *Boius Menalcas:* Menalcas is a commonplace name for a shepherd. *Boius* could refer to "northern" or could also be "Bavarian", as often in the Latin of the humanists.

18. *addis cornua pauperi.* The horn in Roman, as in Hebrew, literature is a symbol of power. After Horace, Ovid wrote, *tum pauper cornua sumit* (*Ars Amat.* 1.239) (then the poor man takes on horns).

20. *militum arma:* Armed clashes of the armies with peasants were frequent during the Thirty Years War. But once again, Balde lifts an entire phrase from Horace *Odes* 3.21.

21. *cocta Ceres:* "cooked Ceres" is beer.

Poem 34

Liber I, Ode XXXIV
Ad Maciem
In die natali
Cum aestivis diebus Eberspargae moraretur

    Soror Galeni, vivida sanitas
    Tibi dicati corporis, huc ades;
        Huc Gratiarum quarta, divis
            Iuncta tribus, Macies, sonoros

5   Molire passus. Ostia pandimus
    Dilecta priscis vatibus ac Deo
        Spirante facundoque plena.
            Flecte meum subitura limen,

    Huc flecte currus. Nil vetitum tuis
10   Videbis usquam legibus: omnia
        Ex arte respondent magistrae,
            Molle nihil tenerumve tactu;

    Non nidor ex abdomine, non adeps
    Cubilis ullo fumat in angulo.
15   Consurgit ex tophis ab imo
            Inque cavum sinuatur arcum

    Ingressus antri; cetera pumice
    Ornantur albo; cardinibus crepat
        Abiegna motis porta; passim
20   Calva iacet solidumque saxum est

Meter: Alcaic strophe

Title: While at Munich, Balde formed a sort of temperance society whose objective was to counteract the principal fault of the German people of that day: excessive eating and drinking.

   At Ebersberg in Upper Bavaria, the Jesuits had a house (the old Benedictine abbey, closed in 1595) that served as a tertianship (third year of probation or noviceship) and a villa.

Book 1, Ode 34
To Thinness
On his birthday
While he spent the summer days at Ebersberg

    O sister of Galen, Miss Gauntness, dear heart,
        Your lover has health quite excessive;
    The Graces, your sisters, a new task impart –
        They soften his footsteps impressive.
5   My portals endeared to the poets of old,
        Are bright with the light of your smiling;
    They're open to you, come enter, behold,
        I long for your visit beguiling.
    You'll see not a thing that's forbid by your law
10   Or opposed to the art of your teaching;
    Nothing soft, nothing tender, no, never a flaw
        That would mar your sprightlier preaching.
    No girth round my stomach of forty or more,
        No fat oozing warm in an angle;
15   And the threshold is formed of an arch o'er the door
        Of rock climbing up in a tangle.
    With pumice stone soft it is mottled in white,
        And the gate made of fir (hear it creaking
    On hinges of death) while my bald head at night
20   Finds its rest on the stony soil reeking.

Text:

1. *Galeni:* Galen was a 2nd century A.D. physician. Over 100 of his medical treatises have come down to us.

3. *Gratiarum quarta:* Balde adds *Macies* to the three Graces *(divis...tribus)*: Aglaia, Euphrosyne, and Thalia.

13. *nidor:* smell, aroma from cooking.

14. *fumat:* the 1643 edition of Balde's odes reads *gliscit*.

20. *calva:* a noun here: "a scalp without hair".

Pulvinar ingens. Querna vel ossea
Vel nulla sedes. Ipse ego corneus
 Et paene tralucens futuri
  Anticipo cinerem sepulcri

25 Praelargus umbrae. Non ego nescio
A te probari tale palatium.
 Invise: iam carmen subactis
  Disposui geniale chordis;

Neu terrearis turbine cimicum
30 In me ruentum lege ferociae:
 Mordere si possunt, acutos
  Et poterunt hebetare dentes.

Intra: quid haeres? tu Polyhymnia,
Tu dulcis olim Terpsichore mihi,
35 Nunc maior ipsamet Minerva et
  Delicium gracilis poetae.

Text:
33. *Polyhymnia:* "She of many songs," one of the Muses, patroness of sacred song.
34. *Terpsichore:* "She who delights in dancing," the Muse of dancing.

    The chairs are of oak and hard as a bone,
        Or none, if you list to my telling;
    And I am translucent with never a tone –
        Like the spiritless souls in their dwelling,
25 I'm worn to a shadow. I know you approve
        Of this palace of mine. Is it hateful?
    I've written some strains, which in minor chords move,
        As my natal day greeting so grateful.
    Oh, be not disturbed by mosquitoes that swarm,
30   With hostile intentions attacking;
    If they bite me they'll blunt their own teeth and not harm
        My skin that is used to their wracking.
    Come enter. Why wait? You were once unto me
        Polyhymnia and mistress of dancing;
35 But now even more than Minerva can be,
        You're the joy of a poet entrancing.

Poem 35

Liber II, Ode VIII
Exclamatio
In funere divitis, cum sepeliretur
Carmen extemporale

Adeste, magni carceris incolae,
Parvoque claudi discite carcere.
   Hanc vestra libertas Seriphum,
     Hos Gyaros subit exul orbis.

5   Post fata cunctis sufficit angulus
    Et parvus asser. Turrigeris ubi
      Innixa Maurorum columnis
        Ac minio variata moles,

    Aut lata per quae iugera milvius
10 Volans citatas tot stadiis tamen
      Lassavit alas? Nunc avitis
        Nomen ubi fluitare bullis

    Sparsum et cruenti sanguis originem
    Foetens tyranni? Nunc lituis ubi
15   Elisus et rumor vapore
        Astra super populosque vectus?

    Venter pusillus, grande negotium,
    Quo iam recessit? Quis leget ostrea
      Gaurana pransuro? Ligatae

---

3. *Cyclad's sands:* Cyclad's rocky strand; 47. *o'er nightly bower:* that over beds lower, and, over death's portals lower.

Meter: Alcaic strophe

Title: An earlier version of the title was, "In the spirit of Gray's *Elegy* – a man's funeral – a dirge".

Poem 35

Book 2, Ode 8
A Dirge
For the funeral of a rich man
A Song Unrehearsed

Come forth, you souls, from far-flung prison lands,
    And learn to be enclosed in prisons small;
Your freedom now will be on Cyclad's sands,
    Confined to place of exile and a pall.
5   When life is done, a little spot for all,
    A little urn will serve, though columns high
Of marble, grace the mausoleum's hall
    And umber tint the walls where you may lie.
Does not the kite that flies over wide domains
10 In longer reaches, wearied, droop his wing?
Will not your name with its heraldic strains,
    Soon cease with boastful voice to ring?
The blood that's sprung from tyrants in their day,
    Its vaunted story voiced with trumpets' blast,
15 Its rumor's lost beyond the starry way,
    Like mist that's scattered, never made to last.
Where now the care you gave that you might dine?
    Who now will gather oysters for your board?
Where is the mouldy cask that held your wine?

Text:

1. *magni carceris:* "our world", "the universe".

2. *parvo...carcere:* "the coffin", "the grave".

3. *Seriphum:* Seriphos, a small rocky island in the Aegean, used by the Romans for exile. The modern name is Sérifo.

4. *Gyaros:* Gyara, like Seriphos, was another one of the Cyclades which was used by the Romans for exile. The name of the island today is Yiaros. Both symbols are borrowed from Juvenal, *Sat.* X.170: *"ut Gyarae clausus scopulis parvaque Seripho".*

19. *Gaurana:* of Mt. Gaurus, now Monte Barbaro. The *ostrea* were oysters from the Lucrine lake. Mt. Gaurus overhangs the Lucrine lake. This verse recalls Juvenal's *Sat.* VIII.85-86: *"cenet licet ostrea centum/Guarana".*

20   Quem veteri saturabit uva
    Fuligo testae? Pomiferis ubi
    Autumnus implens arboribus nemus?
        Funesta creverunt Adami
            (Insere nunc Meliboee) poma.

25 Ingratus heres cetera possidet
    Te flente ridens; ille palatii
        Metator insultat sepulcro,
            Calve, tuo titulosque calcat.

    Fert ille torques et Tyrii vomit
30 Spumas aheni: te redimiculis
        Cingent inornatum lacertae.
            Heliadum bibit ille crustis

    Tandem solutis Caecuba clavibus
    Mappamque tingit: te nec aqua, cinis,
35   Lustrare dignetur. Quietem
            Sub placido capit ille cygno:

    Te saxa pressant. Ille reconditae
    Talenta gazae promet et intimae
        Avarus immigrabit arcae:
40   Funereo tibi nec triente

    In os reposto. Si lacrimas dedit,
    Cum dulce pondus, carum odium, extulit,
        Credantur emptae vel Charontis
            Immemorem redolere Lethen.

45 Pro fluxa rerum, fluxa potentia
    Opumque ludus! somnia, somnia
        Emissa per rimas eburnae
            Mox iterum revocanda portae.

Text:

24. *Meliboee:* Meliboeus, a shepherd in Virgil's *Eclogues* 1 and 7. Balde seems to use the name for "Everyman", though he does cite the beginning of Virgil *Eclog.* 1.74 verbatim.

30. *aheni:* bronze vessel. The term was used of the vessels in which purple color was produced (hence Balde uses the adjective *Tyrii,* Tyrian); but here *Tyrii aheni* seems to mean simply "expensive goblet".

32. *Heliadum:* The Heliades were daughters of Helios who were changed into poplars. Their tears were amber. So *crustae Heliadum* are cups embossed with amber (this is another echo of Juvenal: *Sat.* V.38).

33. *Caecuba:* Caecuban wine from a marshy place in southern Latium.

40. *funereo...triente:* The fare for Charon to cross the Styx. It was placed in the mouth of the deceased.

44. *Lethen:* Lethe, a river of the underworld from which Shades drank and received forgetfulness of the past. "To smell of *(redolere)* Lethe" means the tears are short-lived and soon forgotten.

20   Will they return to satisfy their lord?
        Where is the harvest time, so sweet with breath
           Of ripening fruit upon the bending trees?
        Come, Meloboeus, tell the tale of death,
           That Adam's fruit has left upon our knees.
25   While you're in tears, your heir will smugly smile
           To have your wealth; and in his palace famed
        He'll mock your lowly sepulchre, the while
           He spurns the very titles you once claimed.
        Your diamond-studded collars he will wear,
30   And scatter Tyrian perfume in his stride;
        While lizards crawling over you, stripped and bare,
           Will leave their slimy chaplets as they glide.
        From amber-studded goblets he will sip,
           Your wine brought forth from hidden cellar room
35   Will stain your linens; not one drop will drip
           In sacrificial way upon your tomb.
        Beneath the down he'll take his nightly rest,
           While over your silent grave the stone will press;
        The treasures stored so long in secret chest
40   Are squandered idly and without redress.
        Not even the ferry coin will he bestow.
           The tears that lightly fall at your demise
        Are void of love and every one will know,
           He little thinks of mournful death's disguise.
45   The play of riches and the pomp of power,
           So quick to pass, and all that wealth e'er gave
        Are like the dreams aloft o'er nightly bower
           And not recalled when summoned to the grave.

Poem 36

Liber II, Ode XXII
*Artificiosum simulacrum pusionis
In aditu horti pensilis Albertini*

    Puelle, seu te progenuit novus
    Fictrice vivum Pygmalion manu,
        Sive ipsa praegnantem rosarum
            Postquam uterum dea Flora solvit

5   In huius horti deposuit toro
    Matremque ut ipso munere disceres,
        Priore custodem remoto
            Pensilium dedit esse florum,

    Vincis capillis Earini comas
10   Et ore Nisum. Sangarius tibi
        Suaque deceptus figura et
            Latmius Idaliusque cedunt.

    Tam delicatae verus imaginis
    Optet vocari Praxiteles pater,
15   Suosque perlustrans Amores
            Pinniferum Citherea credat.

    O, ni loquelae fata tibi, puer,
    Usum negassent, quae mihi panderes
        Arcana stellarum recepta
20   Auribus et Satyrorum acuta!

---

6. *placed:* new; 7. *sprawling:* hanging; 11. *no not:* not e'en; 12. *lovelier:* finer; 14. *deft:* sweet; 15. *will:* can; 16. *grander:* lovelier; 18. *tell:* speak;

Meter: Alcaic strophe

Title: The Albert is Prince Albert of Bavaria. The *pensilis* of the title is more accurately translated, "hanging". The gardens were part of Albert's palace in Munich (cf. *Ode* II.20) and were linked to the Jesuit College by means of a covered gallery.

Poem 36

Book 2, Ode 22
A box tree trimmed in the figure of a boy in the formal gardens of Albert

My little lad, did some new artist hand
  Give life to you, or are you sprung
From Flora's womb of roses, thus to stand
  At this grand gate with flowers hung?

5 To learn your mother's charm in that design,
    A guardian placed to watch and care,
  Or scatter perfume from the sprawling vine
    Of burgeoning blossoms clustered there?

  In beauty lovelier than the emperor's slave,
10   Or Nisus e'en in kingly grace;
  Not Atys, not Endymion, no not the knave—
    Young Cupid—has a lovelier face.

  Praxiteles could well the artist be
    Of your deft beauty, and in truth
15 Among her loves will searching Venus see
    No grander Cupid in his youth.

  O, boy, if fate would only not deny
    The use of speech, what secret you could tell
  Of stars that ride over clouds on high,
20   Revealed to satyrs in the dell!

Text:

2. *Pygmalion:* Pygmalion of Cyprus became enamored of a statue he had made. Venus gave life to it at his earnest petition.

4. *Flora:* the goddess of flowers.

9. *Earini:* Earinus, a slave of Domitian. Statius' *Silvae* 3.4 is entitled *Capilli Flavi Earini.* Latmius and Sangarius appear there too (lines 40-41).

10. *Nisum:* Nisus, son of Hyptacus and friend of Euryalus (cf. Virgil, *Aen.* 9.176 ff.). Another possibility is Nisus, king of Megara. His beauty may be based on a lock of purple hair on his head, but Balde does say *ore,* implying facial beauty.

10. *Sangarius:* "of Sa(n)garis", a river in Asia Minor. Balde alludes to Attis, beloved of Cybele, who loved the nymph of the river, Sangaris or Sagaris.

11. *suaque deceptus figura:* Narcissus.

12. *Latmius:* "of Mt. Latmus", a mountain in Caria where Luna kissed Endymion; hence *Latmius* means "Endymion".

14. *Praxiteles:* the celebrated Greek sculptor of the fourth century B.C.

16. *pinniferum:* Cupid (the winged one).

16. *Citherea:* for *Cytherea,* an epithet of Venus. Cythera was an island in the Aegean, celebrated for the worship of Venus.

Nam scis et audis, qualibus area
Dilecta noctu ferveat incolis;
   Vides Napaearum choreas
     Institui saliente Luna.

25 Sic perge dulcis sidereum nemus
(Et istud audes) ingredientibus
   Ad limen arridere; perge
     Sic teneri nive pollicis prae-

libare flores, pulcher ianthini
30 Pincerna veris. Te Zephyritidum
   Fratrem coronabit quotannis
     Et violae linet aura succo.

Text:

23. *Napaearum:* the dell-nymphs.

30. *pincerna:* cup-bearer.

30. *Zephyritidum:* "daughters of Zephyrion", a promontory in Cyprus, an island sacred to Venus. Hence here it means, "daughters or devotees of Venus". Others take it to mean "daughters of Zephyr".

You know so well the nymphs in gay array,
    Upon the sod in festive bands,
As through the night they dance the roundelay,
    Alight with tripping moonbeam strands.

25   Continue then to greet with your sweet smile
    The visitor who comes to view,
And with your flowery fingers to beguile
    With blossoms bright scattered on the dew.

Fair servant from the cup of spring's delight,
30   Pour forth your nectar. Your reward
Will be the West Wind's sisters' light
    To freshen all with perfume nard.

---

20. *in the dell:* hearing true; 27. *flowery:* flowered (and) marble; 28. *with blossoms:* the flowers scattered; 31. *the West Wind's:* the gentle West Wind's; 32. *perfume:* pleasant.

Poem 37

Liber II, Ode XXXIII
Choreae mortuales

Saltemus, socias iungite dexteras:
Iam manes dubius provocat Hesperus;
Per nubes tremulum Cynthia candidis
    Lumen cornibus ingerit.

5   In lodice senes non bene pendula,
In ferruginea cyclade virgines:
Sed picta violis grex tener instita
    Alternos facimus pedes.

Hic et Pontificum ture fragrantibus
10   Rus pastoris olens pileus infulis
Et regum Tyriis paenula vestibus
    Miscentur sine nomine.

Nullus de tumulo sollicitus suo
Aut pompae titulis invidet alteri.
15   Omnes mors variis casibus obruit
    Nullo nobilis ordine.

Nobis nostra tamen sunt quoque sidera,
Sed formosa minus: sunt Zephyri licet
Veris dissimiles auraque tenuior
20   Cupressisque frequens nemus.

Meter: Third Asclepiadean

Title: Earlier sub-titles were "Thoughts" and "A medieval type poem".

Poem 37

Book 2, Ode 33
The Dance of Death

On with the dance! In friendship join your hands.
   The twilight hour summons forth the shades,
   The moon appears through cloud banks' fleecy glades
In lights of silv'ry crescent bands.

5   As old men, in our cloaks not hanging well,
   And maidens in our steel-gray flowing shawls,
   As youthful lads in violet tinted palls,
We trip our dances through the dell.

Here priestly fillet with incense perfume,
10   And shepherd's cap that smells of country farm,
   And royal garment with its Tyrian charm,
Are nameless in their mingled doom.

No one's concerned about his lowly grave
   Or envies ought his closest neighbor's lot,
15   For death has whelmed us all in diverse plot
No ranks the nobles now enslave.

We have our stars, though of a lesser light,
   And different zephyr breezes blow,
   The air is lighter, and the groves we know
20 Are filled with cypresses of night.

Text:

2. *Hesperus:* Hesperus, the evening star.

3. *Cynthia:* Cynthia, here for Luna, the Moon.

5. *lodice:* coverlet, blanket, counterpane; here: a heavy, coarse garment in contrast to the soft, light *cyclade.*

6. *cyclade:* state-robe for women.

7. *instita:* border or flounce of a tunic.

11. *paenula:* mantle worn for journeys and in rainy weather. It contrasts with the rich Tyrian garments.

20. *cupressisque:* The cypress was sacred to Pluto and was used at funerals.

O dulces animae, vita quibus sua
Est exacta, nigris sternite floribus
Quam calcamus humum, spargite lilia
 Fuscis grata coloribus
25 Aptos ut choreis inferimus pedes!
Ut nullo quatitur terra negotio!
Dempta mole leves et sine pondere
 Umbre ludimus alites.

Ter cantum tacito murmure sistimus,
30 Ter nos Elysium vertimus ad polum,
Ter noctis tenebras (stringite lumina)
 Pallenti face rumpimus.

Nos quicumque vides plaudere manibus,
Cantabis similes tu quoque naenias.
35 Quod nunc es, fuimus. Quod sumus, hoc eris.
 Praemissos sequere et vale.

Text:
30. *Elysium...polum:* "the Elysian reign", the abode of the blest. The expression is a mixture of pagan and Christian concepts: the Elysian Fields were situated in the underworld; *polus* refers to heaven (above the world).

O blessed souls, whose life has passed away,
   With dark-hued flowers sprinkle all the lawn
   Where now you dance, and scatter lilies fawn
Full pleasing in their dull array.

25 How sprightly now we pace the dance of death;
   Our earth is troubled by no other deed –
   With weight removed we lightly tread the mead,
In winged shades and airy breath.

Three times we stop our song in silent prayer,
30   And thrice we turn our gaze to heaven's vault,
   And thrice the nightly shade we do assault
With torches of a waning flare.

Oh, you who see us in our ghostly dance
   Will some day sing a similar threnody.
35   What you are now we were and like us you will be.
Farewell! or come along as we advance.

Poem 38

Liber II, Ode XXXVI
Ad Somnum
Quum insomnia laboraret

Mansuete Mortis frater, eburneae
Dynasta portae, non nisi palpebra
    Labente tranquillasque clausis
        Per tenebras oculis vidende,

5   Curas potentem demere mentibus
    O Somne, ramum certius admove
        Et hinc et hinc perfunde tempus
            Rore soporiferaque virga.

    Tu numen almum mitibus influis
10 Succis in artus; tu grave taedium
        Abstergis instaurasque vires
            Mane recens habiles labori.

    Iam laetus ignes elicit Hesperus,
    Iam nox ephebos ordinat aetheris
15   In agmen et Phoebo sororem
            Substituit propiore curru.

    Iamque in pharetras plumigeras avis
    Arguta vocis tela recondidit,
        Glebisque lassati terendis
20   Curva boves referunt aratra.

    Stat mutus orbis; grata silentia
    Exhalat aër: me tamen unicum
        Quietis expertem fatigat
            Triste dolor piceaeque fesso

25 Haerere curae. Quid, placidissime
    Divum, moraris? si tua vel volens
        Vel irretorta fronte sprevi
            Dona sciens, (neque enim recordor)

Meter: Alcaic strophe

Title: Some editions of Balde's poems read the plural *insomniis* in the title. The translation was done by Clare Rooney.

Poem 38

Book 2, Ode 36
To Sleep
When suffering sleeplessness

    Death's gentle brother, who presides
    As monarch of the ivory gate,
    All sight of whom has been denied
    Save through the tranquil shade to eyes
5   held fast by drooping lids' faint weight,

    The wand from mind to banish care
    Endowed, O Sleep, more surely thou
    Move hither, and now here, now there,
    My temples pray bedew with drops distilled
10   by that dream-laden bough.

    O kindly god, thyself let flow
    Within my limbs in healing oil;
    Make heavy tedium to go,
    And in thy morning freshness strength renew
15   adapt for heavy toil.

    Glad Hesperus his starry fires
    Forth heralds now, while night that train
    Of airy soldiery in choirs
    Wheels and Phoebus' sister sets for him
20   in their low-hanging wain.

    The bird, in quiver feather-bound,
    His voice's arrow shrill e'er now
    Has hid; and, wearied by their round
    Of breaking glebe, the oxen yoke are
25   drawing the curving plow.

    All earth stands mute; the air exhales
    A grateful stillness. Me – no part
    Of nature's rest – dark gloom assails
    Alone; and pitchy brood of cares clings fast
30   to my exhausted heart.

Text:

6. *Somne:* Sleep (Hypnos), the son of Nyx (Night) and brother of Thanatos (Death, line 1). Through the ivory gate *(eburneae...portae)* of Hades, Sleep sent false dreams.

13. *Hesperus:* Hesperus, the evening star.

15. *Phoebo:* here: the sun.

15. *sororem:* here: the moon.

Poenas scelestus iam meritas dedi.
30   Placate tandem Somne revertere
         Et innocenti sparge Lethe
             Irriguos vigilantis artus.

Effunde plenis frigora cornibus
Mitique siccum lumen inebria
35   Caelo reclinatumque corpus
             Ossa super line dormientis,

Sed absque rhoncho. Sic tibi Tarquini
Parcente dextra plura papavera
     Crescant in hortis; sic opacet
40   Silva caput chlamydemque et arcam

Natura blandis repleat otiis,
Sed illud antrum, cui Deus incubas,
     Non turbet umbrarum caterva
         Tristis Atlandiadesque Ductor.

45   Sic nulla crudi flamina murmurent
     Apeliotae, nulla tonitrua,
         Stridensve nocturnae volucris
             Penna sonet, penitusque septas

Text:

37. *rhoncho:* snoring, snorting.

37. *Tarquini:* Tarquin the Proud. Balde alludes to the story in Livy (I.55.6-10), according to which Tarquin, wishing to indicate to his son in a silent way that the nobles of Gabii were to be liquidated, cut off the heads of the poppies in his garden.

44. *Atlandiadesque:* a male descendant of King Atlas: Mercury.

46. *Apeliotae:* East Wind

O why, most kindly god of all,
Dost thou delay? If I have spurned
Thy gifts – for I do not recall –
If willfully or consciously my face away
35   from thee I've turned,

It's long, O Sleep, since I have paid
Meet penalty, a guilty knave;
Return thou then, with ire allayed,
These wakeful limbs of mine with Lethe
40   waters dream-infused to lave.

From brimming horns thy coolness send;
Let moisture drop from heaven's grace
Upon my thirsty eyes; and lend
Thy ointment's aid to bony frame which lies
45   at length in sleep's embrace.

Let be no heavy snoring; so –
While Tarquin's heavy hand stay still –
May poppies rife in gardens grow;
May forests furnish for thy head their darkling
50   Shade and nature fill.

Offendat aures; sed fuga rivuli
50   Per prata gratum mobilis obstrepat,
    Et lenis audiri susurrus
        Sub platano trepidantis aurae!

Pro vota! cuius damnor inertiae?
Totus labasco; vix lubet hiscere;
55   Piget moveri. Sella lectus
        Esto: puer, citharam repone.

Purse, cloak with coin of ease. So may
That leader grim, descent who boasts
From Atlas' line, forbear affray
The cave o'er which as god thou standest guard
55   by his array of ghosts;

So may no blasts the East Wind hoarse
Bark forth; no peals of thunder sound
Or bird of night in hissing course
Make discord to assault that inner ear
60   with ramparts girt around.

But let swift-darting streamlet's patter
Through glasslands slip in shimmering flight,
On purling lip light grateful chatter,
And whisper faint to hear through plane tree
65   sign of quivering Zephyr slight.

How now! these vows! To what great sloth
Am I condemned? I'll fall! I say –
I've barely strength to yawn; I'm loth
To move. This chair must be my bed. Here,
70   boy! Come take this harp away.

Poem 39

Liber III, Ode VII
Ad D. Virginem assumptam
In eius pervigilio

Quae est ista, quae ascendit de deserto deliciis affluens, innixa super dilectum suum? Cant. 8.5

    Quo die terris properans relictis
    Tota migrasti super astra Virgo,
    Floribus stratum tibi tergus incur-
        vavit Olympus.

5   Dulce te visa gradiente caeli
    Carmen auditum resonare, Qualis
    Ista per nigrae loca senta silvae et
        Horrida tesqua,

    Qualis ascendit Dea? tota pulchra
10   Gaudiis gemmat liquidis suoque in-
    nixa Dilecto volucres per auras
        Floribus halat!

    Talis in seram, sua regna, noctem
    Luna cum venit, tenuatur Arctos,
15   Pallet Arcturus positoque ferro
        Languet Orion.

    Talis electi speciosus oris
    Phoebus Aurora lacrimante ridet,
    Quando cristatis avibus coruscum
20   Mane precatur.

    Inter has voces magis elevata
    Bracchiis Nati superas id omne,
    Quod Deus non est, animumque toto
        Numine mergis.

25   Merge: dum dulci maris e profundo,
    Quod superfusum bibis, una saltem
    Gutta distillet lacrimasque nostri
        Temperet orbis.

Meter: Sapphic strophe

Title: This translation was also done by Clare Rooney, who simplified the title to "To Mary in her Assumption".

Poem 39

Book 3, Ode 7

To Mary on the vigil of her Assumption

    O Virgin on what day, complete, you went
        In soul and body from this world of ours
    To speed beyond the stars – Olympus bent
        His back for you and covered it with flowers.

5   When rising you were seen by skyey choirs
        Sweet song was heard: "This one who cometh here
    What Lady she, through country spiked with briars
        In darkland wood and over wasteland sere?

    What goddess here ascendeth? All in sheens
10   Of sparkling gems, her beauty washed in showers
    Of joy, she shines. On her beloved she leans
        And through light winging winds she breathes of flowers."

    When such as she has come – the Lady Moon
        To tardy night (her own realm), Arctus fails,
15   Arcturus loses color, and so soon
        His bow laid by, Orion droops and pales.

    Such Phoebus of the handsome face when bright
        He laughs – though at his birth Aurora failed
    To hold her tears – what time young morning's light
20   In splendor's flash by crested birds is hailed.

    Among these voices, lifted by your Son
        In his arms rest, O lifted higher, higher
    Beyond all that which is not God, you've won,
        You dip your soul in godliness entire.

25   So dip: and while you drink of floods which spill
        Their surplus from that sea's sweet-tinctured deep,
    Pray grant us that one drop at least distill
        For tempering the tears our world must weep.

Text:

3. *tergus:* alternate for *tergum,* "back", used for the sake of meter.

6-10. These verses are Balde's paraphrase of the *Canticle of Canticles* 8.5.

8. *tesqua:* Also *tesca:* rough, wild regions sacred to the gods.

14-20. Constellations and Dawn pale before the Moon and Sun respectively.

15. *positoque ferro:* Orion is often depicted with a sword at his side, and Balde seems to allude to this weapon rather than to the bow.

Poem 40

Liber III, Ode XLIII
De spinulo suo

Quod nec psittacus audeat,
    Nec phoenix patrii de cineris rogo
Heres ipse sui, neque
    Iunonis volucer gemmeus impetret,
5 Audes, delicium meum,
    Me turbare canentem imperiosius,
Siren rustica, spinule,
    Ales nequitiae dulcis et ingeni.
Seu furatus amygdalam
10   Pennis, cum repeto, stridulus emicas,
Seu rostro digitum adpetis
    Infusum citharae nec sinis ultimas
Primis iungere vocibus;
    Et quandoque tuam protrahis eclogam.
15 Seu te gurgite proluis
    Et mox unguiculis molle fricas caput,
Ut collo redeat lyra
    Et plumae veteris temperies metri
Concinno super aequore;
20   Quamquam pectine dum comeris, annus est:
Tantum forma negotium,
    Fluctus tot subigis, rursus ut excites.
Huc, o noster, ades nihil
    Virgati metuens carceris ostium:

---

12. *a-flutter:* a-fluttering.

Meter: Second Asclepiadean

Title: *Spinulus* is a diminutive of *spinus,* one of the many genera of finches found almost everywhere on earth.

Poem 40

Book 3, Ode 43
His finch

What never parrot dared to do
    Nor Juno's gem-decked bird,
Nor phoenix rising from the grave,
    You dare – in jest unheard.

5   You rascal, my, how bold you are
    To stop my singing muse.
You rustic siren, naughty finch,
    What is your latest ruse?

Where did you steal that color brown?
10   Stay here, why fly away?
I'm asking – now you peck my hand
    A-flutter in your play.

You mar my harmonizing chords,
    You keep on singing bold,
15   And now you bathe before my eyes –
    Stop splashing or I'll scold.

You preen your crest with claws so soft,
    And ease your feathers down.
What beauty yours! why all the fuss?
20   You need not seek renown.

Come closer now, you need not fear
    The door of willow coop.
You're free to fly throughout the room
    Or skip on reedy hoop.

Text:

4. *Iunonis volucer:* peacock. In Statius' *Silvae* 2.4.26, there is a parallel expression, *"gemmata volucris Iunonis".*

9. *amygdalam:* almond. Here Mertz took it as "almond-colored", and understood *furatus* (having stolen) in a figurative sense. The literal meaning of "having stolen an almond" is much better.

25   Non captivus enim domi,
       Sed saltu teretes per radios vago
    Lascivis in arundine.
       En florem milii: corripe semina,
    Ruris innocuas dapes,
30   At secura necis grataque fercula.
    Sic vivas avibus bonis.
       Post, cum non rigido candida pollice
    Pennam vulserit Atropos,
       (Parcae et vestra secant stamina, si vetus
35   Smyrnae fabula creditur).
       Componam violis mollibus et sacris
    Funus Pieridum rosis.
       Addam perpetuum serta virentia,
    Donec Melpomene soror
40   Parnassi riguis collibus inferat.

Text:

27. *lascivis:* a verb here: "you frolic".

28. *milii:* millet, which is a kind of grain.

33. *Atropos:* "She who is not to be turned", one of the three Parcae (line 34) or Fates.

35. *Smyrnae fabula:* Balde alludes to the fact that Smyrna was the reputed birthplace of Homer. Thus the expression is equivalent to "the Homeric tale".

37. *Pieridum:* the Muses.

39. *Melpomene:* Melpomene, the muse of tragic and lyric poetry.

25	Come, take the grain! I offer, see,
	The prize grain of the field;
	It's your best food and helpful too
	To be 'gainst death a shield.

Be good and live your life serene.
30   And when with clammy hand,
Old Atropos will pluck your wing
    (If this old tale still stand),

I'll bury you deep in violets,
    And sacred roses soft,
35 I'll call the muses to your grave,
    To lift your soul aloft.

I'll plant the ivy o'er your mound,
    Fit due your many trills,
And then with dear Melpomene
40   You'll live on lyric hills.

---

28. *to...shield:* 'gainst bitter death your shield; also, to be from death a shield.

Poem 41

Liber IV, Ode XLVIII
Heliotropum
sive mens hominis ad Deum versa

      Iamque adeo toti nutu pendemus ab uno,
         Alea iacta semel.
      Numinis imperio commisimus omnia: tanti
         Sit retinere nihil.
5   Iusserit: in Libycis stivam ducemus arenis
         Caucaseove iugo.
      Iusserit: Ionia remos lentabimus unda
         Carpathioque freto.
      Observent timidi mergum fulicasque marinas,
10   Quid meditentur aves
      Litoreae, fallax quo vento strideat aer,
         Quid nova luna coquat,
      An tristes vultu protendat lurida nimbos,
         Anne serena micet,
15   Dormiat, an refluum vesano concita cornu
         Arietet Oceanum.
      Si Deus ire monet, numquam retinebit Orion
         Nubilus inter aquas,
      Ut gladio findat mediae fundamina navis,
20   Tutior asser erit.

---

6. *make:* plough.

Meter: First (minor) Archilochian system (dactylic hexameter followed by dactylic catalectic trimeter)

Title: Balde wrote this poem on the occasion of his final vows, July 31, 1640. Heliotrope can be used for any plant that turns toward the sun or, more specifically, it is the turnsole. As the subtitle shows, Balde used the heliotrope as a symbol of the mind seeking its God.

Poem 41

Book 4, Ode 48

The Heliotrope – the mind of man turned to God

    In deep submission to the will of God
        I've vowed my all;
    To his control I've left each act
        Without recall.
5   Should he command – on Libyan sands
        I'd make my way,
    Or on Ionian Sea I'd set my sails
        And anchors weigh.
    Let timid souls look on the dangers dark
10   That lie ahead;
    I'll view the care-free gulls maneuvering
        Far overhead.
    What matters it whence blow the stormy winds,
        Or what new fear
15   The moon in misty veil portrays, or threat
        In clouds appear.
    If God should call, not e'en Orion's sword
        Would frighten me
    Nor keep me from embarking on a raft
20   In choppy sea.

Text:

3. ff.: Balde refers to the abnegation of self-will and self-determination through obedience.

5. *stivan ducemus arenis:* Plowing sand is a secular, classical image for the monastic "watering a dry stick", an activity that only blind obedience would perform. Balde may also allude to the fact that he could be sent anywhere (Africa, Caucasus, Ionia, or the Aegean).

7. *remos lentabimus:* we will ply the oars.

9. *Carpathio freto:* The Carpathian Sea around the island of Scarpanto between Crete and Rhodes.

9. *mergum fulicasque marinas:* "the diver and the coot". These birds predict storms at sea. The two are mentioned together at Ovid, *Meta.* 8.635, but not precisely as predictors of rain.

10-11. *aves litoreae:* "wading birds" in distinction to the marine birds above.

12. *coquat:* "cooks" in a metaphorical sense: "to contrive, to meditate upon, to plan".

16. *arietet:* "butt like a ram"; in a metaphorical sense: "to disturb, to harass, to disquiet".

17. *Orion:* Boeotian hunter, changed into a constellation in the northern skies.

Sed neque Phoebeis aetatem metiar annis,
    Pendulus a radio.
Ille meas quo non alter formosior, horas
    Temperat, ille meus
25 Sol maior parvique faber totoque videndus
    Altior axe scopus.
Huc desiderium iaculetur pectoris arcus,
    Quanta pharetra patet.
Certior huc pleno, quo meta remotior, ictu
30   Nostra sagitta volat.

Text:

21. *Phoebeis...annis:* Phoebean years are time measured according to our human life on earth (reckoned in "suns"). Balde in contrast reckons time by measuring it with God *(ille...quo non alter formosior).*

25. *parvique faber:* "the fashioner of small things".

26. *scopus:* "goal", "target". It is a very rare word in classical Latin. Cicero used it as a Greek word in *Ad Att.* VIII.11.2.

I shall not measure life by months and years
   In God's embrace,
For he will soothe the hours, as he notes
   Each single trace
25 Of my good will, submissive to his own
   In love's requite.
I'll safely live; my goal is fixed in God
   Who leads aright.

Poem 42

Liber IV, Ode XLIX
Ad Virginem Matrem
Pro euthanasia sive felici morte
Carmen votivum

O Diva, vitae praeses et altera
Spes vatis, olim cui mea me super
    Servum dicavi; da, priusquam
        Fata citent oculosque claudant,

5   Da poenitentes et lacrimas sacro
    Dolore laetas in mare Creticum
        Quascumque proiectura noxas.
           Tum tenera mea fila dextra

    Abscinde, Virgo; neu fragilem colum
10 Tres fabulosae praecipitent anus;
        Diffido. Tu devolve nostram,
           Iure tuam potiore lanam.

    Hoc esto votum, sic precor ultima
    Ex cordis urna vita fluat, meus
15   Sic stagnet in maioris aevi
           Oceanum gracilesque bullas

    Aeternitati misceat Isara.
    Sic elabora, sic bene praepara
        Perambulandum luctuosae
20   Mortis iter placidoque somno

Meter: Alcaic strophe

Title: "A Votive Song" is a later addition. At the end of his translation, Mertz wrote, "The classical allusions have more or less been dropped, or rather modified." A few years after the publication of this ode, Fr. Vincent Caraffa, S.J., General of the Society of Jesus, petitioned for and received approval of the Bona Mors Society (1648).

Poem 42

Book 4, Ode 49
To the Blessed Virgin for a Happy Death
A Votive Song

    O Lady, thou my guide and second hope,
    To whom I've vowed myself a serf to be,
    Grant ere the angels close my eyes in death,

    That penitential tears from contrite heart
5   Wash in the ocean of God's mercy
    All stains of wayward years.

    Do thou then, Lady, cut the tender thread;
    Weave thou from tangled yarn
    A finer tapestry of love and fear.

10 Be this my prayer: let life flow forth
    From my heart's urn into the sea
    Of limitless eternity.

    Guide thou its way, as in a pleasant dream,
    Through labyrinthine halls of death
15 To rest eternal.

    May one man offer thee his wealth,
    Or build a shrine; another lay
    His gifts upon thy sanctuary floor.

Text:

4. *citent:* "summon to judgment". The verb *citare* was used as a synonym for *in ius vocare,* the first step in a Roman civil trial.

6. *in mare Creticum:* "as many tears as drops of water in the Cretan sea". There seems no reason for Balde to choose this sea over any other except for the fact that Horace's *Carm.* 1.26.2 has the exact same phrase in the same place of the line in an Alcaic strophe. There, too, the phrase is used for any large body of water.

8. *fila:* "thread (of life)." This is a frequent usage in the poets.

10. *tres fabulosae...anus:* "the three fabled crones" are the three Fates.

14. *meus:* modifies *Isara,* a masculine noun, meaning the Isère river in Gaul. Balde uses the Isère as a symbol of life's flow, merging itself into the Ocean of eternity. It is a learned reminiscence of a passage of Lucan, *Bellum Civile,* I.399-401. There the Isère is described as a river which loses itself in a greater one.

15. *sic stagnet:* "May my (heart) be inundated into the Ocean of a greater age". May he pass to eternal life.

16. *Isara:* This is the Latin form of no fewer than four rivers in Europe. As indicated in the note for line 14, the reference here is to the Isère in Gaul.

Compone manes. Hi voveant opes
Aedemque ponant, caedat hic impares
   Agnos pavimentumque sparsis
     Visceribus linat hostiarum:

25   Ast ipse supplex, ipse ego taeniam
Gestabo vittasque: ipse tibi cadam
   Evincta circum fronde lauri
     Victima procubitura ad aras.

Text:

21-24. The subjunctives in this stanza could also be taken as jussives. "Let them vow", "Let them place." These actions would be to placate and to win longer lives. Not so for Balde (*Ast ipse*, "But I..."). He is dressed as a victim and will fall before Mary's altar.

       But I, on bended knee
20   With sacrificial fillet in my hand,
       Will fall beneath the stroke of death,
       A victim at thy altar's shrine.

Poem 43

Liber VII, Silviludium XVII
Ad Petrum Altenhofium

Auctor de mortuali feretro sibi prospicit: supervacaneam epitaphiorum curam et pompam irridet.

    Quid? si beatis Mentibus asseri
    Indulget Aether, PETRE, caristia
      E rupe decisas sepulchri
        Pyramides, Pariamque molem

5 Quaeremus Umbris? Frangite marmora
    Distincta venis; tollite lugubrem
      Fastum, redundantesque pennas
        Funeris et titulos, Amici.

    Offendor istis: HEIC. IACET. ARMAGRA,
10 MARDO. CARALLUS. VASCO. PERONIUS.
      TRIUMVIR. EXCONSUL. SENATOR
        CONSILIO. MANIBUSQUE. MILES.

    TER. AD. POLONOS. AD. LIGURES. QUATER.
15 QUATER. BRITANNOS. MISSUS. AD. ULTIMOS.
      LEGATUS EXTREMUM. VIENNAE.
        SOLE. DIEM. MORIENTE. CLAUSIT.

    At ecce circum sesquipedalibus
    Caelata signis, pendet imaginum
      In gentis armorumque laudem
20   Pompa ferox, galeaeque et enses

Meter: Alcaic strophe

Title: An individual poem of the *Silvae* was called a *Silviludium*.

Poem 43

Book 7, Silviludium 17
To Peter Altenhof

The author despises all funeral pomp and ceremony.

If a kind Providence has placed us among the blessed, why do we look for pyramids of stone and Parian marble over the shades of the dead? (5)

Smash your mottled marble, away with the display of grief and the multiplied funeral titles and decorations. (10)

I hate to read: HERE LIES THE KNIGHT MARDO, A COUNCILMAN, EX-CONSUL, SENATOR, SECRETARY OF THE ARMY.

THREE TIMES AMBASSADOR TO POLAND, FOUR TIMES TO NORTHERN ITALY, FOUR TIMES TO FAR-OFF BRITAIN, CLOSING HIS LIFE AT VIENNA AT THE SETTING OF THE SUN. (15)

And all around there are engravings in bronze a foot-and-a-half high, and a wild display of crest and shield and helmet and swords. (20)

Text:

2. *caristia:* alternate for *charistia,* an annual family repast taken three days after the Parentalia on February 20, a family banquet at which feuds were settled. Hence the meaning, reconciliation.

4. *Pariamque molem:* Parian marble, a white stone used for monuments (here: *decisas sepulcri Pyramides*).

7. *pennas funeris:* "the feathers of the funeral", that is, the fluff and pomp of the rite.

17-18. *sesquipedalibus...signis:* "foot-and-a-half figures" on the tomb's bas-relief.

18-20: *imaginum...pompa:* Like the Romans of old, the 17th century Germans boast of their ancestors' accomplishments (line 19: *in gentis laudem*).

Cristaeque et umbo: monte super tigris,
Supraque scutum vultur, et aurei
　　Caput coronatum leonis
　　　　In medio; Libycique dentes,
25　Cervique cornu. Scilicet ut sciam
Fuisse nuper PUS generosius
　　Hac sede defossum. Facesse
　　　　Flebilium miserande luxus.

Odi sepultae marmora gloriae.
30　Foetent in urna grandia nomina.
　　Incestat et Manes cadaver,
　　　　Quod sub humo putridum superbit.

Me, si paratum, PETRE, iubentibus
Suprema Fatis hora citaverit:
35　　Longam quidem, sed impolita
　　　　Sandalipam fabricabis orno.

A fronte scribis: HEIC. IACET. ALSATA.
POETA. QUONDAM. NON. SINE. LAUREIS.
　　O vanitas! expunge rursus,
40　　*Si iaceam,* satis est, *quiete.*

Text:

24. *Libycique dentes:* Libyan teeth are ivory tusks.

36. *sandalipam:* a bier for people of the lower classes.

40. *iaceam...quiete:* is the new inscription. It is enough for Balde if he "rests in peace".

On the shield a tiger stands on the mountain and in the center there is the crowned head of a golden lion with ivory and horn.

And all that can be seen is a complete decomposition in the grave, the sad display of passing splendor.

I hate marble slabs of past glory; great names rot in urns. (30) The body which tries to be proud decomposes under the ground.

Peter, when my last call comes, prepare for me a simple undecorated coffin. (35)

On the front write: HERE LIES AN ALSATIAN POET, ONCE NOT WITHOUT HIS LAURELS. It's all vanity! Blot it out! If I lie in peace that is all I want. (40)

René Rapin
(1621-1687)

Jesuit Poet, Critic, and Controversialist

René Rapin, French humanist and controversialist, was born at Tours at November 3, 1621. At almost eighteen years of age, he entered the Society of Jesus on October 22, 1639. After teaching literature and oratory for nine years at Tours and Paris, he devoted the rest of his life and his whole apostolic endeavors to writing. In Latin poetry, an early production, the *Eclogae Sacrae (Sacred Eclogues),* won for him the accolade of the "Second Theocritus". His acknowledged masterpiece, *Hortorum Libri IV (Four Books on Gardens),* imitates Virgil's *Georgics* and treats respectively: flowers (Bk. I), groves (Bk. II), water sources (Bk. III), and fruit tree orchards (Bk. IV). The initial edition (Paris, 1665) is a handsome publication with exquisite woodcuts. The work has seen many subsequent editions and was translated into English twice (London, 1673; Cambridge, 1706). It was also translated into Italian and French. Critics have acclaimed the work as worthy of comparison with those of the masters of the Augustan age.

Rapin was even more prolific as an essayist in the French language. One major division of his work was literary criticism. His most noteworthy efforts here are *Observations on the Poems of Horace and Virgil* (1669) and *Reflections on the Poetics of Aristotle and on the Works of the Poets, Ancient and Modern* (1676). As especially the first title indicates, Rapin favored comparisons of the classical Greek and Roman authors. Hence we find in his other essays, comparisons of Demosthenes and Cicero, Plato and Aristotle, and Thucydides and Livy. These comparisons were also translated into English as early as the 17th century.

In the fields of ascetical theology and controversial literature, Rapin's chief works were *The Spirit of Christianity* (1672) and *The Perfection of Christianity* (1673). Although a lifelong foe of the Jansenists, Rapin's chief controversial works were not published until the nineteenth century. One of his editors ascribes the reason for Rapin's not publishing the works during his lifetime to Rapin's perfectionism and to a desire on the author's part to spare the families of those attacked in the works. His two posthumous works are *History of Jansenism,* edited by Domenech (Paris, 1861) and *Memoirs on the Church, Society, the Court, the City, and Jansenism,* edited by Aubineau (Paris, 1865). Despite the late appearance in print of these works, Rapin's chief place in theology was his role as antagonist to the Jansenists.

After a long and fruitful career as poet, literary critic, and controversial theologian, René Rapin died at Paris on October 27, 1687.

Poem 44

Ode III
Ad Cicadam

    O quae virenti graminis in toro
    Cicada blande sidis, et herbidos
        Saltus oberras otiosos
            Ingeniosa ciere cantus.

5   Seu forte adultis floribus incubas,
    Caeli caducis ebria fletibus;
        Gaudesve persultare campi
            Graminei virides per undas,

    Seu voce concors accinis aemula,
10 Pagi eruditas inter arundines;
        Aut provocatos cantilenis
            Agricolas animosa vincis;

    Seu per loquaces garrula rivulos
    Stridore rauco ludis agrestibus
15   Lassis, fatigatisque bobus,
            In medio modulamen aestu;

    Exaggerati seu tibi nectaris
    Rorem ministris perpluit imbribus
        Caelum, coronatosque gemmis
20   Roriferis thalamos adornet;

    Ades canenti; dum tibi marmore
    Vates perenni, carminibus bonus
        Molitur immortale templum,
            Unde per ora virum volabis.

Meter: Alcaic strophe

Title: Mertz originally wrote, "Thoughts for a suggested lyric".

Poem 44

Ode 3
To a Cicada

Dear cicada, so happy in your home on the meadows of green fields, you skip over the quiet grasses to sing your song!

Whether you alight on a full-blown flower, (5) wet with the dew of the morn, or whether you spiral along over the waves of moving grain, whether you pour out your song and challenge others in the listening reeds, (10) full of life, you regale the tired farm worker and refresh the weary oxen (15) in the noontide heat.

May heaven give you whole showers of nectar and adorn your resting place with heavenly jewels and dews from on high. (20)

To me, the poet, your song suggests a lasting marble temple through which your voice will sound and bring joy to the hearts of men.

Text:

5. *adultis floribus:* "flowers in full bloom".
6. *caeli caducis...fletibus:* "the tears fallen from the sky" are dew or dew-drops.
9. *accinis:* "you sing with".
10. *eruditas...arundines:* "learned pipes". That is, pipes of shepherds whose songs the cicada rivals.
13-16. The verb in this stanza is *ludis.*
15. *bobus:* dative plural of *bos,* ox; usually *bubus.*
16. *modulamen:* melody, euphony.
21-24. With this poem, Rapin fashions an immortality for the cicada.

EPITOME ANNALIVM TREVIRENSIVM

QVA ANTIQUÆ URBIS AC DIOECESIS *TREVERICÆ*, IN POLITICO ET ECCLESIASTICO REGIMINE EXORDIA, PROGRESSÚSQUE, AC RES BELLO AC PACE ADMINISTRATÆ, BREVI CLAROQUE ORdine digestæ sunt, cum aliis Romani Imperii Gestis eidem conjunctis.

PER R.P. JACOBUM MASENIUM è SOCIETATE JESU.

Anno  1676.

Augustæ Trevirorum, typis & sumptibus Christophori Wilhelmi Reulandt.

Jesuit Poet and Historian

Jacob Masen
(1606-1681)

Jacob Masen was born on March 23, 1606, in Dahlem in the old duchy of Jülich (Rhineland). We hear of Masen's playing four parts in the *Stephanus,* a play put on by the Jesuit college at Köln in 1627. He pursued his studies there all the way to the Master of Arts degree. Thereafter, he entered the Lower Rhine province of the Society of Jesus at Trier on May 14, 1629 at the mature age of twenty-three. His career as a regent, theologian, and young priest is hard to trace exactly and most of the information is based upon inferences made from remarks in the introductions to his works. For a total of some fourteen years, Masen taught poetry and rhetoric at Emmerich, Köln, Münster, and Aachen. On May 3, 1648, Masen pronounced his final vows at Köln. There followed after his literary career, a long and distinguished apostolate as preacher at Köln, Paderborn, and Trier. Masen spent his final days at Köln where he died on September 27, 1681.

For almost thirty years there was a steady stream of writings from the pen of Jacob Masen. Biographers have classified Masen's works in various ways, but in general they fall into the following four classes: 1. poetry; 2. rhetoric; 3. history; and 4. asceticism. The poetic works include epigrams, odes, epics, and his most significant works, dramas, where he was a standard-bearer in Jesuit theater. The lyric pieces in the present anthology are taken from an early collection (1650) entitled, *Speculum imaginum veritatis occultae (A Mirror with Images of Hidden Truth).* Among the epics, the *Sarcotis,* which describes the fall of man, may have had some influence on Milton's *Paradise Lost,* though no one today holds with the Scotsman, William Lauder (1753), that Milton plagiarized Masen. In dramatic poetry, seven plays have come down to us and it is in this area of dramatic poetry that Masen has most made his mark. One play, however, was not so successful. In 1647, Masen put on his play, the *Androphilus,* at Münster in an effort to calm the students who were agitated by the events and personages surrounding the Peace of Westphalia (1648). It affected little and the student disturbances continued. Other plays were the *Ollaria (The Pot,* in imitation of Plautus' *Pot of Gold*) and *Mauritius, Orientis imperator (Maurice, the Emperor of the East),* a story of the conversion of a Byzantine emperor.

Masen also wrote extensively on the theory of poetry in his *Palaestra eloquentiae ligatae (Arena of Poetic Eloquence)* in three volumes. Volume I treats of poetry in general; Volume II takes up elegy, lyric, and epic (the *Sarcotis* is found here); and Volume III studies dramatic poetry.

In the field of rhetoric, in addition to his sermons published in the *Orthodoxi Concionatoris (The Orthodox Preacher),* Masen wrote on the theory of public speaking in *Palaestra oratoria (Arena of Oratory)* and *Palaestra styli Romani (Arena of Roman Style).* As an historian, Masen's most important contribution was the completion of Christopher Brower, S.J.'s history of the diocese of Trier. Masen edited Brower's work and added the last three books of the 25 volumes in the *Antiquitates et Annales Trevirenses (The Antiquities and Annals of Trier).* A few years after the publication of this work, Masen produced an epitome of it. In the area of asceticism, Masen's chief work was the *Dux viae ad vitam (The Leader on the Way to Life).* The work consists of meditations and other exercises inspired by Ignatius' *Spiritual Exercises* and is meant to help both lay persons and clerics/religious in their quests for holiness. The *Aurum Sapientiae (The Gold of Wisdom)* has an interesting theme described by its subtitle, *Ars sine scelere et cum virtute ditescendi (The Art of Getting Rich without Crime and Virtuously).*

Toward the end of his life, Masen remarked to a fellow Jesuit that he had spent his life in such a way that he devoted every available moment to the glory of God and the good of his neighbor. Surely the large number of publications and their wide scope justify Masen's claim to diligence.

Poem 45

Ode V

Ad Paulum Russum,
In extremo adhuc senio stulte opibus inhiantem

     Quis credat? stygio proximus ostio
     Et dextro feretrum iam subiens pede,
        Partum defodit aurum
           Antro Russus inutili?

5   Quo praemittis opum fulva cadavera
     Mox ibis socius. Desine, Manibus
        His praeludere curis,
           Nec vivo loculum instrue.

     Sic est: iam dubiis ora coloribus
10 Livent caerulea mortis imagine,
        Iam contractior atram
           Sulcat ruga cuticulam.

     Iam torpent hebetum spicula dentium,
     Genuinique fluunt. Dic, age, quis tua
15   Quis iam commolet, amplis
           Quae congesseris horreis?

     De naso tepidis stiria guttulis
     Irrorat gremium perpetuis tuum.
        Albet barba pruinis,
20   Fulget nulla serenitas.

---

1. *gates of death:* the mouth of the Styx; 7. *anticipate your own death:* dig your own grave; 7. *don't take on:* with all; 10. *signs of death:* the image of death; 20. *is seen:* is detected.

Meter: 5th Asclepiadean

Title: Mertz's original title for this piece was, "The Miser (a paraphrase)". That describes more accurately what he did, for this is not a translation. On the theme and tone of the poem, Mertz commented, "This is a rather gloomy picture but Shakespeare has 'Last scene of all,/ That ends this strange eventful history,/Is second childishness, and mere oblivion,/Sans teeth, sans eyes, sans taste, sans everything.' *(As You Like It,* II.7.163-66)."

Poem 45

Ode 5

To Paul Russus
A stupid old man who still longs for money

Who'd believe it? Here's an old man – his name is Russ – close to the gates of death, with his right foot practically under his own coffin, digging up his hoarded and useless gold.

To whom do you promise this corpse of yellow metal? (5) Don't anticipate your own death, don't take on the cares of the gloomy sisters.

The fact is there. The changing hues of bluish tints on your face are signs of death (10) – the deep ruts in the tightened skin, the blunted teeth, the drooling mouth.

Come, tell us who'll get what you have gathered in your big barns. (15) Your nose drips on your breast, your beard is white with the frosts of winter and nary a smile is seen. (20) . . .

Text:

2. *feretrum:* bier, litter. To use a colloquial expression, Masen is saying that Russus "has one foot in the grave".

3. *defodit:* buries in the earth.

5. *opum fulva cadavera:* "the golden shambles of riches" is a bold metaphor to underline the futility of burying treasure.

13. *spicula dentium:* points or edges of the teeth.

14. *genuinique (dentes):* jaw teeth, back teeth.

15. *commolet:* grind thoroughly, a rare, but classical word.

17. *stiria:* Literally, an icicle; but here it means, dripping, dribbling.

18. *irrorat:* moistens, besprinkles.

Subsidit patulis palpebra vallibus,
Infaustoque rubent lumina sanguine,
   Urget denique tardas
     Aures plumbea surditas.

25 Procurrit medio frons tibi vertice,
Totum vix satis est debile synciput:
   Quantum frons tibi crescit,
     Tantum de cerebro perit.

Fallit planta suis ebria gressibus
30 Et vultus dubiis omnia nutibus
   In contraria torquens,
     Laevo denegat omine.

Vix tandem solidi pars superest viri.
Quod vitae reliquum est, hoc male prodigit,
35 Hoc vel possidet olla,
     Vel concluditur horreis.

Russus nempe diu vivere desiit,
Decepitque necem. Funeris ultimi
   Pellem praeter et ossa
40   Nullae relliquiae manent.

Text:

26. *synciput:* also *sinciput:* brain, head.

30-31: Masen describes the shaking head of the elderly that causes distortion in visual perception.

32. *laevo...omine:* In the language of augurs, *laevus* meant "fortunate, lucky, propitious" since the Romans turned their faces to the south and had the eastern signs on their left.

40. *relliquiae:* Poetic spelling for *reliquiae,* which lengthens the quantity of the first syllable.

... Your eyelids flutter, your head is constantly trembling and your brain shrinks in proportion as your baldness increases. (25) Your step is unsteady like a drunkard's, and hardly a single trace remains of what man really is. (30) What is left is fit only for an urn (35) or to be left in your bank box.

Russ gave up living long ago. He fooled death. Only skin and bones are left for a funeral. (40)

---

36. *to be left:* left; 36. *bank box:* bank account.

Poem 46

Ode XIII

Cupiditatem excellentiae hominem despicabilem reddere

      Mollis vellere serici,
         Et pictam Phrygio stamine cycladem,
      Et sparsum femoralibus
         Argentum remove, nec muliebriter
5   Comptum surrige verticem,
         Elatoque forum schemate Iulium
      Personatus obambula:
         Contemptim reliquos spernere contumax.
      Torva nube supercili
10   Et sperni reliquis intolerabilis.
      Res est caeca superbia,
         Quamvis Argi oculos, Lyncis acumina,
      Serpentisque Epidaurii
         Certet perspicuo vincere lumine:
15 Quamvis ambitiosior
         Spectari populo praetereuntium
      Signarique levi manu;
         Quamvis Assyriis grandior atriis,
      Et vulgo famulantium,
20   Et rerum Dominis praesideat viris:
      Res abiecta superbia est:
         Quamvis Sidoniis picta coloribus
      Longo syrmate vestium
         Pavonis superet gemmea fimbrias:

Meter: 3rd Asclepiadean

Title: *Cupiditatem excellentiae:* "Desire for excellence" is a mild version of the poem's theme, which is pride, haughtiness.

Poem 46

Ode 13

Pride lowers the dignity of man.

Put away your silks and satins
And silver decorations,
And don't parade like a Caesar
In the forum with head trimmed like a woman, (5)
And despise the rest of the folk with a cynical eye.
Pride is a blind thing, (11)
Though it is overanxious to see
With the eyes of Argos,
With the sharp vision of the lynx,
Or the snake of Epidaurus;
To be seen by the passerby –(15)
And the slight wave of the hand –
And be honored as an Eastern potentate.
Pride is a contemptible thing, (20)
Though it show itself in colors of Sidon
And is distinguished by its cloak of grandeur
And gem-studded dress like a peacock.

Text:

2. *Phrygio stamine:* with purple thread.

3. *femoralibus:* covers for the thigh. *Femorale* is a late word and rare.

5. *surrige:* lift up.

6. *schemate:* here it means "posture, mien".

6. *forum...Iulium:* the Julian Forum was one of the three principal places of public business in Rome (the other two were the Roman Forum and the Forum of Augustus). Masen means "public life".

12. *Argi:* Argus, the hundred-eyed keeper of Io.

12. *Lyncis:* The *lynx* was noted for its eyesight and its keenness was transferred to Lynceus, son of Aphareus, one of the Argonauts. He, too, was famed for the sharpness of his sight.

13. *serpentis Epidauri:* "The serpent of Epidaurus" was a snake sacred to Aesculapius, who had a shrine at Epidaurus. The Greeks fancifully connected the noun *drakon* (snake) with the verb *derkomai* (I see).

18. *Assyriis...atriis:* Assyrian courts are majestic meeting halls.

22. *Sidoniis...coloribus:* Sidonian (or Phoenician) colors are purple.

23. *syrmate:* a robe with a train. It was worn especially by tragic actors.

25   Res est foeda superbia.
        Quamvis ingenii dotibus abdita
    Pervadat sapientiae, et
        Multarum titulis polleat artium;
    Res est stulta superbia,
30   Quamvis Sithonias, fronte super nives
    Cerustata retineat,
        Cincinnosque vibrans verticis aureos,
    Crines vincat Adonidis:
        Sic ornata, caret fronte superbia
35   Quamvis turgida sensibus
        Fumosas proavum iactet imagines,
    Factorumque recens decus
        Et grandis titulorum aura reconditum
    Inflet pectoris ambitum;
40   Sic elata, caret mente superbia.
    Faustum submove inutilem,
        Ut multis placeas, nec placeas tibi.

Text:

30. *Sithonias...nives:* snows of Sithonia, a region in Thrace, famous for its snow.

31. *cerustata:* "colored with white-lead". The form is a late Latin alternate for *cerussata*.

32. *cincinnos:* locks of curled hair.

33. *Adonidis:* Adonis was beloved of Venus for his extraordinary beauty, part of which was due to his golden hair.

42. The last line is in Italics in the printed editions and is meant to be a proverb, "In order to please many, do not be self-satisfied".

Pride is an ugly thing, (25)
Even though it has all the marks of genius
And the character of many arts.
Pride is a foolish thing.
Though it may retain the beauty of face (30)
And the well-groomed hair of an Adonis,
Even so Pride lacks countenance –
Even though it boast of ancestral armory (35)
And recent deeds performed with glory.
Pride is really insanity. (40)
Replace a useless promoter
That you may please many
And not just yourself.

Jesuit Poet and Virgilian Scholar

Charles de la Rue
(1643-1725)

Charles de la Rue (Ruaeus) was born in Paris on August 3, 1643. As a sixteen-year-old, he entered the Society of Jesus on September 7, 1659. He was to spend 65 years in the Society until his death in 1725. The early part of his career he spent in teaching humanities and rhetoric at the College of Louis the Great of Paris. Pierre Corneille paid de la Rue (or the King) the compliment of translating into French some of his Latin poems, celebrating Louis XIV's victories over the Dutch and the Bavarians. From this period dates the beginning of de la Rue's work in drama. He wrote a *Lysimachus,* a story placed in the time of Pyrrhus of Epirus, and a *Cyrus,* a story that he derived from Herodotus and Justinus. To the more strictly literary part of de la Rue's career belongs the extensive commentary on the major works of Virgil. The explanatory notes, rhetorical exercises, and indices were produced as an aid to the Dauphin, and as such saw many editions in the famous Delphin series. Our selection is from a group of emblematic poems that de la Rue addressed to various leading French citizens.

As did many of the Jesuits whose poetry appears in this collection, so too, de la Rue became a court preacher and confessor/spiritual director to the nobility. He enjoyed a great reputation as a preacher, and many of his publications were speeches, especially funeral orations. Although immersed in court life, de la Rue longed to go to Canada and to labor among the North American Indians as a missionary. His superiors, however, would only allow him a brief mission of three years duration to Languedoc and the area of the Cévennes.

At the advanced age of 82, Charles de la Rue, distinguished Latinist, humanist, and court preacher passed away in Paris on May 27, 1725.

Poem 47

Symbola Heroica
AD NOBILES GALLOS
Regis Exemplo Invictos
Aquilae in Solem Defixae
Lemma
Crescunt vires animique tuendo.

    Quod et procellas inter et aspera
    Deproeliantum murmura fulminum,
        Dum cuncta terrarum tremiscunt,
            Impavida volitamus ala;

5   Quod aemularum protinus alitum
    Se turba nostris viribus imparem
        Non erubescenda fatetur
            Sponte fuga, domitisque late

    Decedit auris: non patrium genus,
10 Non celsa summis e nemorum iugis
        Origo, non acres dederunt
            Indomitae stimuli iuventae.

    Ipse, ipse tantos addidit impetus,
    Quem terra curru gaudet in igneo
15   Fulgere sublimem, et remotis
            Pallida nox veneratur umbris.

    Hinc ille totis artibus emicat
    Fervetque venis aetherius vigor.
        Phoebaea tanti est irretortis
20   Lumina luminibus tueri.

Meter: Alcaic strophe

Title: The printed symbol or emblem in the 1693 edition of de la Rue's poems reads *videndo,* not *tuendo.* The meaning is virtually unchanged though *tuendo* does suggest a longer, more steady gaze. The lemma does read *tuendo.* The King in question is Louis XIV, *Le Roi Soleil,* the Sun King.

Poem 47

For the Nobility of France, like their King, unconquered: An Escutcheon: Eagles with their eyes fixed on the sun and the motto, "strength and courage grow by watching".

In the midst of all the storms and hazards of war alarms, with the world in travail, we fly along securely. (4)

Let every other group which tries to keep on equal footing with us declare honestly, without blushing, that it is unequal to the task and depart from our shores. (9)

It is not the heritage of our ancestors, not the product of our mountain groves, not the inspiration of the enthusiastic young – (12)

He it is! he, who like the sun on high, rides sublimely in golden glory, and even night is brightened with all shadows removed. (16)

He shines forth in all the arts. A power, as if from heaven, radiates abroad and we look at the sun's glory with untroubled eyes. (20)

Text:

3. *Virgil at Aen.* 5.694-5 wrote, *"tremescunt/Ardua terrarum". Tremisco* is an alternate spelling of *tremesco.*

4. *volitamus:* we hover, we flutter.

13. *Ipse, ipse:* the king, Louis XIV.

19-20. *irretortis...luminibus:* with unflinching eyes.

20. The 1693 edition notes that this poem and other emblems that follow were dedicated to Louis XIV on August 13, 1679 in the Society's Paris college named after that king.

Noel Étienne Sanadon
(1676-1733)

Noel Étienne Sanadon was born at Rouen, France, on February 16, 1676. Influenced no doubt by the example of his Jesuit uncle, Nicholas Sanadon, Noel entered the Society of Jesus at the age of fifteen on September 8, 1691. Sanadon taught humanities at Caen for his regency, but the lion's share of his apostolic life was to be spent at the Louis the Great College, where he taught rhetoric from 1711 until 1718 and was a fellow teacher of the famous P. de la Porée who taught so many of the 18th century French authors, both Jesuit and lay. On February 2, 1711, Sanadon pronounced his final vows in the Society of Jesus at Louis the Great College in Paris.

After 1718 a change was called for in Sanadon's life and he went to Tours where he functioned as a prefect of studies. It was during this time at Tours that Sanadon finished his translation and edition of Horace's *Odes* and *Epodes*. The edition caused quite a stir at the time since Sanadon drastically altered the arrangement of the poems and divided and combined them. Sanadon's French translations of the poems had lasting effect, but the editorial work was soon abandoned. His year-by-year life of Horace has also perdured.

In 1728 Sanadon was called back to Paris and the Louis the Great College to serve as librarian. He held this post until 1732, when his health turned for the worse. He passed away the next year at Paris on October 22.

In addition to the translation and edition of Horace mentioned above, Sanadon published a collection of his own poetry in 1715 under the title *Carminum libri IV.* Book 1 contains lyric poems, the first ode of which praises the Jesuit Latin poets; Book 2 has elegiac poems; Book 3 epigrams; and Book 4 contains miscellaneous pieces. There is also a Book 5, which Sanadon entitled *Liber Adventitius (Added Book);* it consists of translations into French and Greek. Finally a posthumous work on geography for beginners was published in 1744.

The life and work of Noel Étienne Sanadon were wrapped up in his duties as teacher and administrator. His published works are either texts of some sort for students of poetry and rhetoric or are occasional pieces to commemorate visits of Louis XIV, Louis XV, and other dignitaries to the Jesuit college. As in both our selections, so in most of his work, Sanadon imitates classical models and the results of his labor won his contemporaries' esteem of him as one of the most eminent Latin poets of the age.

Jesuit Poet and Horatian Scholar

Poem 48

Liber III, Epigramma II
In Mortem Passeris

Lugete, O Charites, Ioci, Lepores,
Et quantum est volucrum venustiorum,
Et quantum est iuvenum pudentiorum.
Passer Thyrsidis innocens voluptas,
5   Unum suaviolum, una cura passer,
Nunc heu! frigidus inquilinus Orci
Umbris occubuit tenebricosis.
Non illum malus abstulit rapaci
Rostro milvus, aut scelesta feles
10   Mollem praedam agili occupavit ungue.
Insontem volucrem necavit ales
Implumis, nisi qua leves lacertis
Aptatas gerit hinc et inde pennas.
Nostis quis fuerit molestus ales?
15   Ipse est pessimus alitum Cupido,
Milvis improbiorque, felibusque,
Qui colludere passeri solebat,
Atque una pueri in sinum volabat,
Et circum petulante vectus ala
20   Quaerebat tenerum ustulare pectus.
Sed victus rabie maligniori
Ipsam funere perdidit volucrem,
Quum posset domino nihil nocere.

---

1. *and all you Pleasures and Charms:* with your joys and charms; 4. *source of joy and sweet kisses:* source of pleasure and sweet comfort; 15. *scoundrel:* wicked.

Meter: Hendecasyllabic or Phalaecean

Title: The ordinary translation of *passer* is sparrow. That Sanadon closely imitates Catullus *Carm.* 3, especially at the beginning of the poem, there can be no doubt. There are Catullan echoes throughout the poem.

Poem 48

Book 3, Epigram 2
On the Death of a Canary

Weep your tears, dear Graces all, and all you Pleasures and Charms. If possible, let all birds of rich plumage and young hearts of innocence come and weep.

The canary of Thyrsis, always a source of joy and sweet kisses, (5) is now, alas, an inhabitant of Hades, a victim of dark shades.

No kite with hooked bill, no criminal cat with sharp claws stole him. (10) It was an unplumed bird, who had a feather decoration on his shoulders -you know who it was. It was the scoundrel Cupid, (15) more criminal than any kite or cat. It was he who played occasionally with the canary. It used to fly to the boy with fluttering wing and keep whirling around, looking for a warm spot on his bosom. (20)

But angered with a deadlier malice, he killed the bird because he could not kill its mistress.

Text:

2. Sanadon substitutes *volcrum* for *hominum,* otherwise this line exactly reproduces Catullus 3.2

4. *Thyrsidis:* Thyrsis is the name of a shepherd in Virgil's *Eclog.* 7.2.

5. *suaviolum:* little kiss; here it is used in a transferred sense for "sweetheart, darling". Catullus (poem 99) is the only classical author to use the word, but it is common in the verse of the humanists.

9. *milvus:* the kite is a bird of prey.

10. *ungue:* of an animal: claw; of a bird: talon.

19. *petulante vectus...ala:* borne on playful wing.

20. *ustulare:* to scorch, to singe.

23. *domino:* the Thyrsis of line 4; Mertz mistakenly translated, "mistress", possibly with Catullus' Lesbia in mind.

Poem 49

Liber I, Ode XXVI
Cupido ab apicula punctus
Ex Graeco Anacreontis, Od. 35

    Dum per vireta Cypri
    Rosas legit Cupido,
    Latens apis tenellas
    Pupugit manus puelli,

5   Ille eiulans parentem
    Celeri petit volatu.
    "Heus! occidi, occidi" inquit,
    "Serpens mihi volucris
    (Apem vocant coloni)
10   Plagam intulit cruentam."

    Tunc illa, "nate", dixit,
    "Si tam grave creavit
    Tibi alitis pusillae
    Aculeus dolorem,
15   Quantum putas dolere
    Quos igneis sagittis
    Tibi ludus est ferire?"

---

5. *crying loudly:* bellowing; 13. *little insect:* stinging insect; 15-17. *how much:* how many...to suffer.

Meter: Iambic dimeter catalectic, used rarely in classical Latin, and more frequently in late Latin and in Christian authors.

Title: As the Latin indicates, Sanadon closely imitates Anacreon's poem −35 in M.L. West's 1984 Teubner edition.

Poem 49

Book 1, Ode 26
Cupid Stung by a Bee

While Cupid was picking roses in a garden on Cyprus, a bee, hidden in the bush, stung the hand of the little boy. Crying loudly, (5) he ran to his mother and said, "I'm dying, I'm dying. A snake (the inhabitants call stinging insects by this name) has inflicted a bloody wound". (10)

Venus, in her turn, said, "My dear son, if a little insect can give you such pain, how much pain do you think (15) you cause with your fiery darts?"

Text:

1. *vireta:* variant of *virecta,* meaning "greensward".

4. *pupugit:* perfect of *pungo,* I stung, I bit.

8. *serpens...volucris:* "Flying serpent" was the farmers' name for the bee *(Apem vocant coloni).*

13-14. *alitis pusillae aculeus:* the sting of the tiny winged creature.

17. *ludus:* mere sport, child's play.

PATRUM SOCIETATIS JESU

Ad

RHENUM INFERIOREM

POEMATA

SELECTIORA

Hactenus partim edita, partim inedita: nunc in artis Poëticæ Candidatorum gratiam unum in Corpus congesta, aucta, notisque illustrata

à

FRIDERICO REIFFENBERGIO
ejusdem Societatis Presbytero

TOM. I.

Cum Privilegio Cæsareo, & permissu Superiorum.

COLONIÆ AGRIPPINÆ
Sumptibus THOMÆ ODENDALL Bibliopolæ
Sub pingui Gallina, Vulgo: Unter fetten
Hennen. MDCCLVIII.

An Early Collection of Jesuit Latin Poets

Daniel Ramus
(1676-1733)

Daniel Ramus was born at Trondheim in Norway in July of 1685. He entered the Lower Rhine Province of the Society of Jesus on December 2, 1709 at Trier. For his regency, Ramus taught humanities at Koblenz and subsequently spent most of his apostolic life teaching philosophy and theology at Köln. His elegiac poetry was not published until Reiffenberg's 1758 edition of *Patrum Societatis Iesu ad Rhenum inferiorem poemata (Poems of the Fathers of the Lower Rhine Province)*. Ramus' only other publications were a 1723 philosophical work on primary and secondary causes and a contribution *De sanctorum cultu (On the Veneration of Saints),* published in Zaccaria's *Thesaurus Theologicus* at Köln in 1750.

Daniel Ramus died on October 14, 1761.

Poem 50

Paraphrasis
In Mortem Psittaci

    Humanae solers imitator, psittace, linguae!
        Dux volucrum, et Domini ludicra cura tui!
    Quis tua tam subito praeclusit murmura fato?
        Ante diem vacua stat tibi Parca colo.
5   Illane venturae dederas praesagia mortis,
        Nobiscum hesternas iussus inire dapes?
    Dulcia consuetae repetentem munera mensae
        Pascebat Domini raptus ab ore cibus.
    Quin etiam mediae volitans plus tempore noctis
10   Garrulus es vigiles visus obire thoros.
    Insuper affatus, meditataque verba canorus
        Reddebas, nostros rostro imitante sonos.
    At modo te stygiae lethaea silentia sedis,
        Humanae fallax vocis imago, tenent.
15   Prisca fides sileat: Phaëthontia fabula cedat;
        Nec sua iam solus funera cantet olor.
    Sed tibi quanta domus, rutila testudine fulgens!
        Quos auri radios textile nectit ebur!
    Illa tuo quondam stridentia limina cornu,
20   Nunc querulo raucum carmine sponte sonant.
    Aula suo cantore vacat: vacat ille beatus
        Carcer, et augustae iurgia nulla domus.
    Huc omnis coeat doctarum turba volucrum,
        Iura quibus fandi sors magis aequa dedit.

---

1. *voice:* tongue; 10. *in your visits:* as you visited; 11. *kept up:* repeating.

Meter: Elegiac distich

Title: The fuller Latin title is *Paraphrasis Epicedii statiani (A paraphrase of a Statian dirge)*. Ramus imitates Statius' *Silvae* 2.4 very closely and copies many phrases verbatim. The original Statian poem, however, is entirely in hexameters. Exact verbal echoes are too numerous to cite. Putting a classical poem into another meter was very popular in the 17th/18th centuries. Jacob Vande Walle among the Jesuit Latin poets wrote many such paraphrases.

Poem 50

Paraphrase
Death of a Parrot

Parrot dear, you skillful mimic of the human voice, champion of all birds and my steady, cheerful companion. Who was it that, with dark design, so suddenly stopped your chatterings? Parca is standing by with idle distaff before the designated day of doom. Did you give her some little inkling of your death? (5) Why, only yesterday you had your meals with me when you snatched sweet bits from my plate. You even flew about the greater part of the night, chattering and keeping up your harmonious melody in your visits to my bed (10) and all the while kept up the sounds I taught you. When I spoke to you, you answered with your well-studied phrases. And now there is nothing but the deadly silence of the Styx and only the memory of your human voice. The old song will be silent, the story of Phaëthon heard no more. (15) Let the swan alone remain as the singer.

The house was alight with your bright black feathers, interwoven with ivory and gold – now silent with no complaining voice. Its every corner once resounded with your staccato note. (20) The hall misses its singer, the cage its occupant.

Text:

3. *praeclusit murmura:* has hushed your chirping.

4. *Parca:* the Fate measuring out the thread of life is Lachesis.

13. *stygiae lethaea silentia sedis:* "Lethe's silence in the Stygian hall". The shades drink of the river Lethe and forget all the past.

14. *fallax...imago:* Ramus addresses the parrot who only sounds human, but is not in fact.

15. *Phaëthontia fabula:* Phaëthon lost control of the sun's steeds and was struck down by a thunderbolt of Zeus.

16. Ramus and Statius before him allude to the myth that swans sense death and lament it beforehand.

17. *testudine:* here: overlay, veneer.

19. *cornu:* could be "bill", "beak" or in a transferred sense, "horn", "trumpet".

25   Plangat Phoebeus, plangat Iovis armiger ales,
       Tuque datos facilis reddere, sturne, sonos
    Quaeque refers iungens iterata vocabula perdix,
       Bistonioque soror, quae gemis orba toro!
    Ferte simul gemitus, cognataque ducite flammis
30   Funera, et hoc omnes discite carmen aves:
    "Occidit ille plagae viridis regnator Eoae
       Psittacus, aligeri gloria prima chori
    Quem neque stellatus Iunonis vinceret ales,
       Nec tu Phasiacae rare natator aquae."
35   Ille salutator Regum, titulosque locutus
       Caesaris: et Domini nomina blanda sui.
    Ille loquax, queruli toties vice functus amici,
       Et toties longis certa medela moris;
    Occidit, heu! stygiis tamen haud inglorius umbris
40   Mittitur. Exsequias nobile funus habet.
    Tristes Assyrio cineres adolentur amomo,
       Plumaque Sicanios spirat odora crocos.
    Atque novux phoenix, senii sed inutilis expers
       Praebet Achaemeniis ossa cremanda rogis.

Text:

25. *Phoebeus...ales:* raven.

25. *Iovis...ales:* eagle.

28. *Bistonio...toro:* Thracian couch, from the Bistones, a Thracian people. Tereus, Philomela's violator, was a Thracian.

28. *soror...orba:* Philomela, who was changed into a nightingale.

33. *Iunonis...ales:* peacock.

34. *Phasiacae...natator aquae:* pheasant. The Phasis is a river in Colchis.

41. *Assyrio...amomo:* balm from Assyria.

42. *Sicanios...crocos:* saffron from Sicily.

44. *Achaemeniis...rogis:* Persian (or Asiatic) pyres, so called from Achaemenes, grandfather of Cyrus.

Let the whole flock of learned birds come together, those to whom nature gave the power of speech. Let the bird of dawn, let Jove's eagle, (25) and the starling and the quail and the partridge and the swallow with its moaning, deprived as it is of a home, come to the bier and learn the dirge. (30)

The parrot died, that supreme ruler of the green fields of the East, the glory of his race, more beautiful than Juno's star-flecked bird or even Colchian pheasants. He the greeter of kings (35) and his master's simple pet, always talking and filling in his master's complaints but always a balm in the long depressing moods. He is dead, alas! but scarce sent inglorious to the Stygian shades. (40) His funeral will be marked with perfume of Sicilian nard and Assyrian incense; and a new phoenix, one who lived life to the full, will later give his bones to be burned on Persian pyre.

---

43. *one who lived life to the full:* who knows no useless old age.

The Latin La Fontaine

François J.T. Desbillons
(1711-1789)

François Desbillons was born on January 8, 1711 at Châteauneuf-sur-Cher (Formerly in the duchy of Berry, now the departement of the Cher). He studied at the Jesuit college at Bourges and subsequently entered the Society of Jesus on September 21, 1727. He taught humanities and rhetoric at the Jesuit colleges of Nevers, Bourges, Caen, and La Flèche. However, Desbillons is most closely linked with the Louis the Great College in Paris, where he taught for fifteen years and served as librarian even longer (1745-1762). In the face of the suppression of the Society of Jesus and the various pressures put to bear upon its former members, Desbillons, after brief stays in various French cities, accepted Count Palatine Karl Theodor's invitation and took up residence at Mannheim on the Rhine in 1764. He brought with him his considerable library (at the time of his death, 23,000 volumes mostly of 17th and 18th century French publications), which became the nucleus of the college library at Mannheim. Desbillons died in that city on March 17, 1789.

Desbillons' literary efforts cover a variety of genres, but he is most famous for his fables. Some of his contemporaries referred to him as the "Latin La Fontaine". A major work was a collection of Aesopian fables published in various editions until the 1768 version in 15 books to which Desbillons added some 170 of his own fables to those of Aesop, Phaedrus, and other fabulists. A lasting contribution in the area of ascetical theology was Desbillons' edition of the Latin text of the *Imitation of Christ*. Some of his personal anguish and sadness at the suppression of the Society of Jesus is seen in the late works, *Avis exul (Exiled Bird), Ars bene valendi (The Art of Being Well),* and the iambic poem *Carmen de Pace Christiana (Poem on Christian Peace).* In his day, Desbillons was considered an accomplished Latinist and prominent intellectual.

Poem 51

XIII

Novus Orpheus

De nocte quidam subditus Amoris iugo
Hispanus aegra lacrimabundus lyra
Duras puellae supplicabat ad fores.
At illa blandum miseri amatoris melos
5   Saxis repente depluentibus obruit;
Saltem obruisse credidit; sed musicus
Pulsa canit adhuc obstinatius lyra;
Retroque cedens gradibus ad numeros graves
Bene temperatis: "Orpheus ego pol novus",
10 Dixit, "canoris saxa qui traham sonis".

Meter: Iambic trimeter

Title: Although Orpheus is more commonly thought of as charming wild beasts and the monsters of the underworld, still his musical powers extended to the rocks of Olympus and the Symplegades at the entrance of the Euxine. Thus Desbillons may fittingly describe the Spanish lover as a "new Orpheus".

Poem 51

13

The New Orpheus

The night brought out the Spaniard,
A lover with his flute
To serenade his lady
At portals which stayed mute.

5   But suddenly she answered
With stones thrown from above,
She thought she had dispatched him,
But he renewed his love.

He sang as he departed,
10   In accents loud and strong,
"I'm now a new-born Orpheus
Who lured the rocks with song".

Text:

2. *lacrimabundus:* bursting into tears, with tears.

2. *aegra lyra:* with sad lyre.

7. *adhuc obstinatius:* the more resolutely, all the more stubbornly.

9. *bene temperatis:* well adapted, fitting well.

9. *Orpheus:* Desbillons points out in a footnote that *-eus* is not always a diphthong.

Jesuit Poet and Rector of the Greek College

Tarquinio Galluzzi
(1574-1649)

Tarquinio Galluzzi was born in 1574 at Montebuono in the Sabine country. He entered the Society of Jesus at the age of sixteen on November 11, 1590. Almost all his apostolic endeavors were expended in the city of Rome. There for ten years, he was a professor of rhetoric and for four years he taught ethics. In 1631 Galluzzi was made rector of the Greek College, one of six national colleges in Rome directed by the Jesuits, and he held that position for 18 years until his death in 1649. He passed away at Rome on July 28 at the age of 75.

Galluzzi's poetry was among his earlier endeavors. He published *Carminum libri tres (Three Books of Poems)* in 1611, and the work saw several editions in the 17th century. The three books are divided thus: Book 1: *Heroicorum;* Book 2: *Elegiarum;* Book 3: *Odarum et Epigrammatum.* He also contributed to the revision of the Latin hymns in the Roman breviary which was ordered by Pope Urban VIII and finally completed in 1629.

Galluzzi was a noted orator in his day, and he was called upon to deliver the funeral orations for Cardinal Ossati, Cardinal Bellarmine, and other prominent personages. Galluzzi also worked in the area of philosophy as his translation and commentary on Aristotle's *Nicomachean Ethics* (1632) illustrate.

Galluzzi was highly regarded by both Italian and French authors of his day for his eloquence and erudition. Certainly his original Latin poems and his commentaries on Virgil and other classical Latin authors show a mastery of his models.

Poem 52

Liber III.XXII
De Torquato Tasso poeta primi nominis tumulo carente

Sic, Torquate, iaces merito sine honore sepulchri?
　　Tantus, Tasse, cinis sic tumulandus erat?
Marmor ubi, Pariusve lapis citreaeve tabellae,
　　Nominaque insigni conspicienda nota?
5　Nimirum nullo capitur tua fama sepulcro:
　　Te bene qui posset condere nullus erat.

---

1. *without its:* deprived of;　4. *plaque:* token;　6. *the monument you deserve:* proper burial.

Meter: Elegiac distich

Title: Galluzzi honors the poet Torquato Tasso (1544-1595). Tasso was a very early pupil of the Jesuits, having studied with them at Naples from 1552 to 1554.

Poem 52

Book 3, 22
On Torquato Tasso's Grave

Torquato, is this your resting place without its well-deserved honor?
Could your noble ashes, O Tasso, be thus entombed?
Where is the Parian marble, where are the citrus wood inlays,
Where the plaque that lists your works?
Your great fame can be enshrined in no tomb, (5)
And no one can give you the monument you deserve.

Text:

2. *tumulandus:* to be covered with a mound, to be buried, to be entombed.

4. *insigni...nota:* a record of accomplishment, a laudatory inscription.

5-6. Torquato's reputation and accomplishment surpass any effort to express them with an inscription in stone.

6. *condere:* can mean "to inter", "to bury", and does so here. "There was no one who could bury you as well as you deserved."

Poem 53

Liber III.XXIII

De Veteri Urbe Roma Disiecta

Vidimus Oenotrias arces, eversa duello
  Vidimus in cineres saxa Latina leves.
Nimirum in seros pestis fluit illa nepotes:
  Dardanus hac heres peste necandus erat.
5 Teucria sic fuerat, Teucri sic Roma Quirini
  Debuit in cineres succubuisse suos.

Meter: Elegiac distich

Poem 53

Book 3, 23
The Ruins of Ancient Rome

We have seen triumphal arches of the Wine Country overthrown in war. We have seen Latin monuments leveled flat in small pieces of broken ruins. The calamity, alas, has fallen upon our own grandsons.

But could Dardan's heir be destroyed by this calamity? Could Troy, could the Trojan nobles, (5) be overwhelmed in their own dust?

Text:

1. *Oenotrias arces:* the Oenotrian citadels are the ruins of ancient Rome. Oenotria was the name of the extreme south-eastern part of Italy. Mertz's translation reflects one of the suggested etymologies of the word, "from the best wine".

1. *duello:* the archaic, poetic form of *bello* is needed to fit the meter.

3. *seros...nepotes:* the late descendants are the Romans of Galluzzi's time.

3. *pestis...illa:* "that famous affliction" was the one that destroyed Troy.

4. *Dardanus...heres:* the heir of Dardanus is the contemporary Roman.

5. *Teucria:* Troy.

5. *Quirini:* Romulus. He is called Teucrian because he is descended from Trojan Aeneas.

Poem 54

Liber III.XXIV
In Urbem Novam

Imperium sine fine datum tibi Roma perenne est:
  Pulchrior e quanto funere ducta redis?
Et crescis per damna, ulmus velut icta bipenni,
  Caesaque, fecundo vulnere, plura paris;
5 Est tanti cecidisse tuum, Roma inclyta, tanti:
  Si stares, esses, Roma superba, minor.

Meter: Elegiac distich

Poem 54

Book 3, 24
To the New Rome

Government, great Rome, is yours forever! How much more beautiful do you return to life from every defeat! You grow stronger with every damage sustained. Like an elm cut by the blade of an ax you show greater growth with every wound inflicted. O great Rome! What a gain to have fallen! (5) Had you survived you would be a less great Rome.

Text:

1. *imperium sine fine datum:* Galluzzi deliberately echoes Virgil, *Aen.* 1.279: *imperium sine fine dedi* (I have given rule without end). Galluzzi refers to a commonplace: the new Rome, Christian and pontifical, was built with the stones of the old pagan city.

5-6. Galluzzi presses the paradox that Rome is somehow greater in her fall than she would be if she were still standing.

A Versatile Poet

Vincenzo Guiniggi
(1588-1653)

Vincenzo Guiniggi was born in 1588 at Lucca in Tuscany. He entered the Society of Jesus at the very young age of 13 in 1601. He taught rhetoric at the Roman College with success and was appointed by Fr. Mucius Vitelleschi, Superior General of the Society, to be his personal secretary. The previous two holders of that position (Nicholas Orlandini and Francesco Sacchini) as part of their duties, worked on a detailed history of the Society of Jesus. The work eventually encompassed six large volumes and was not completed until 1859. It brought the history of the Society up to 1633. Guiniggi worked on this history, but was really not a major contributor. For 12 years, however, Guiniggi did fulfill the duties of Fr. Vitelleschi's personal secretary (1625-37). Toward the end of his life, Guiniggi had to bear the burden of almost complete deafness. This affliction he bore to the edification of his fellow religious and finally passed away in Rome on March 4, 1653.

Guiniggi's literary heritage is two-fold. We have some of his orations and lectures delivered, for the most part, at the Roman college, under the title *Allocutiones gymnasticae (Addresses in the Gymnasium),* Rome 1636. This publication also includes the earliest edition of most of Guiniggi's poetry (the drama is missing). His poetry has seen several reprintings and excerpted versions. The collection of poetic works includes dactylic verses, elegiacs, lyrics, epigrams, and the one drama on Ignatius at Monserrat. Our selections are all epigrams. Guiniggi's verse shows a polish and variety of form that mark the Jesuit Latin poets.

Poem 55

Epigramma XXXVII
In Funambulum

    Quis novus hic caelo suspendit Daedalus alas?
        Sed vereor, ne sors Icaron esse probet.
    Aspicis, ut tenui feliciter audet in aura;
        Ceu subeat stabili ludicra bella solo?
5   Fune super tereti tutissimus errat, et artem
        Ludere dum gestit, luditur arte timor.
    Hic choreas impune ciet, seseque supinum
        Librat, et intorto turbine corpus agit:
    Argutat pedibus, tremuloque per aëra saltu
10   Tollitur; erectus sed tamen inde redit.
    Nec mora, nec requies; iterum ter pectus in altum
        Surgit, et in gyrum ter vaga membra rotat.
    Corpore dum pendet, sola cervice tenet se,
        Et vere ad restim colla redacta gerit.
15   Tum simulat casum; populoque timente, timorem
        Ridet qui populi vota timere facit;
    Quin, capite obverso, totus pede pendet ab uno;
        Dumque pedem absolvit, dextera supplet opem.
    Iam iam casurus redit, incertumque theatrum,
20   Quas iubet in partes, speque metuque trahit.

Meter: Elegiac distich

Title: The *funambulus* or rope dancer was a popular street entertainer in antiquity and later.

Poem 55

Epigram 37
The Tightrope Walker

Who is this new Daedalus who spreads his wings in the sky? I'm afraid he will suffer the lot of Icarus.

You see how cheerfully daring he goes through his many tricks aloft as if he were on solid ground. He walks with absolute safety on the tightrope (5) showing his skill. All fear is lost in the art. Now he will strike up a dance and then he'll balance himself lying flat. He makes a complete turn. He kicks his feet, makes a complete sommersault and comes upright to do the turn three times. (10)

There's no stopping his acrobatics. He hangs by his neck and then comes back to the upper side of the rope. He pretends to fall and laughs at the panic of the crowd. (15) As he hangs head down on one foot or helping himself to release his foot, he draws the attention of thousands as he pretends to fall. He's not the only one hanging there – thousands are hanging from the rope with him. (20)

Text:

1. *Daedalus:* famous Athenian architect and inventor.

2. *Icaron:* Icarus, Daedalus' unfortunate son, who ventured too close to the sun. Guiniggi is afraid the tightrope walker will fall.

3. *feliciter audet:* he takes chances with happy outcome; cf. Horace, *Epist.* 2.1.166, where the very same words are used.

4. *ludicra bella:* mock battles, make-believe wars.

8. *intorto turbine:* with the shift in the wind.

9. *argutat:* stomps, stamps.

11-12. The rope dancer makes a triple spin in the air.

14. The body hangs by the neck from the rope.

17. *capite obverso:* with his head turned toward the ground.

18. *dextera supplet opem:* The tightrope walker clings to the rope with his right hand as he frees the grip of his foot *(dum pedem absolvit).*

>   Nec solus pendet; sed enim pendentia secum
>   Uno ex fune tenet milia multa virum,
>   O viles animae, et venalia pectora parvo;
>   Saepe quibus merces esse ruina solet:
> 25 Non sat terra vias habet et divortia leti;
>   Ut iuvet in caelo quaerere mortis iter?
>   An semper vobis subeunda pericula census,
>   Atque omnis fundus denique funis erit?
>   Cum restim aspicitis protensam, dicite: Forsan
> 30   Ultima iam vitae linea ducta meae est.

Text:

23-24. The poet complains of a certain vulgar blood-thirstiness in the spectators; or, perhaps better, of a reckless venality in the performers, whose reward for their daring is often a fall.

25. *divortia:* Here it has the rare meaning of divisions, varieties.

27. *census:* here, as often, "wealth", "riches".

28. *omnis fundus:* all your property, all your possessions. Is your estate to be identified with a mere rope *(funis)*?

Oh, the poor people who are here for such cheap exploitation. The reward is often complete loss. Are there not enough side roads of death on the solid earth? (25) Why do you have to look for death in the sky?

Do you have to meet such dangers to supplement your pocketbook or your land? In the end will all your land be the strand? When you look at it stretched out before you, remember: it may be the last strand of your life. (30)

---

23. *exploitation:* salesmanship; 28. *land:* estate.

Poem 56

Epigram LXIV
De Cicada ad lyram canente

    Pulsabat digitis lyram lyristes,
    Cum fides, male passa verberantem
    Nervo dissiliente dissecatur.
    At cicadula, mens canora silvae,
5   Aestatis melopaea garrientis,
    Iacturam fidis ambitu fideli
    Et dulcis vice vocis implet ultro.
    Nam, lyram superinsidens disertam,
    Pro cassa fide sufficit, locatque
10 Vocem dulciloquae necessitati.
    Sic se temperat ad canentis usum,
    Ut quidquid digitis canit lyristes,
    Illud ore cicada prosequatur.
    Miraris, vice chordulae cicadam
15 Totum provehere et iuvare cantum?
    Tanto verius id mihi probatur,
    Quantum voce propinqua chorda cordi est.
    Ergo desine fabulam putare,
    Hanc, quae tota cor esset, esse chordam.
20 Imo, quo mage sit gemella chordae;
    Cui vicaria iam fuit canendo:
    Huic vicaria sit simul cadendo:
    Par fato, velut ore; nam, repente
    Ruptis faucibus, in lyram recumbit
25 Infelix, nisi sortiatur urnam,
    Qua carent, sed et invident olores.

---

3. *gave no:* never.

Meter: Hendecasyllabic or Phalaecean

Title: Mertz considered sub-titles such as "A Suggested Parallel" and "The Poem Rethought". The version he produced is free, but picks up most of Guiniggi's allusions.

Poem 56

Epigram 64

A Cicada Singing to the Lyre

The lyrist was playing his lyre,
When a string snapped in two on his lute,
But the cricket gave no thought to retire
Though the song of the lyrist was mute.

5   It seated itself on the lyre
And chirped more loudly and strong
His chanson which we always admire,
For the cricket is Muse of the song.

You wonder how the cricket could carry
10   The tune the lyrist had lost?
Remember his little heart merry,
Is song in the sun at all cost.

Don't fancy this merely a story
But truth, if your heart is alive;
15   No lute will supply the full glory,
Where heart and good motives connive.

The music of cricket and singer
Is ended with shadows of night,
No summery noises now linger
20   As the stars dot the heavens with light.

Text:

1. *lyristes:* lute-player. The word is transliterated from the Greek and is used in Silver Age Latin only.

2. *verberantem:* lashing, flogging, drubbing. The word implies rough treatment of the lyre.

4. *cicadula:* This diminutive, whose meaning is obvious, is not found in the standard dictionaries of classical and medieval Latin.

5. *melopaea:* musical composition, song. The word is derived from the Greek *melopoios,* lyric poet, maker of song. Hence, here it means "songstress".

9. *pro cassa fide:* for the useless lyre.

10. *dulciloquae:* sweet speaking; from *dulciloquus,* a late Latin word and a rare one. The epithet is transferred from "voice" to "necessity".

14. *chordulae:* This diminutive is very rare in classical Latin.

17. *propinqua chorda cordi est:* The cicada sings from the heart.

22. *simul cadendo:* The lyre, lyrist, and cicada will all pass away.

26. *olores:* swans. Guiniggi seems to interpret the swans' death dirge as an expression of a desire for immortality.

Poem 57

Epigram LXV
Tumulus Anni Morientis

Hic iaceo, rigidae prostratus vulnere mortis
  Dum mihi quam reliquis augeo, vita perit.
Vivendi merces moriendi debita traxit:
  Et quae vitae aliis, est mihi causa necis.
5 Nempe Deum vidi; Vitam vidisse iacentem
  Arguor, et lucis crimina nocte luo.
Hac tamen ingentem solabor sorte dolorem,
  Non poteram fato splendidiore mori.
Nam quibus in cunis oritur Deus, occidit annus:
10 Sic Domini thalamum sortior in tumulum.
Vita nec amisit, melius sed transtulit usum:
  Dulce mihi heredem lucis habere Deum.

---

6. *sins:* daily sins; 12. *life's:* evening's.
Meter: Elegiac distich

Poem 57

Epigram 65

The Tomb of the Dying Year

    It's here I lie, the victim of stark death;
      The life I give to men is my demise.
    The price of living is for all bleak death;
      The life I give is cause of death to me.
5   I've looked on God, life lying in a crib;
      I, guilty now, atone at night my sins.
    A source of joy in my most bitter grief:
      My fondest hope to die in penitential love.
    For those new born with Christ in manger stall
10   Will meet with greater strength within Christ's grave
    Where life is won and now with better use
      As heir of God in life's sweet repose.

Text:

2. *augeo:* I increase. The old year increases life for others by adding one year to their total of years or, in the spiritual vein of the poem, by having the feast of Christmas at its end (lines 5-6). The end is thus a beginning.

6. *arguor:* I am accused.

6. *nocte luo:* "I pay with night", that is, the old year passes away and yields to the increasing light of the new year.

10. *thalamum...tumulum:* The *thalamus* is the crib in which Jesus lay; the *tumulus* is the tomb of the dying year. Mertz read and translated *fortior,* "with greater strength". The letters *f* and *s* have been confused and the correct reading is *sortior,* "I receive by lot".

LIBER TERTIVS. SOCIETAS AGENS. 471
Scholæ Humaniorum litterarum.

Luditque fauis immista iuuentus.

Narcissi lacrymas, fundamina prima fauorum,
    Corticis & lentum quærite gluten, apes.
Sugite materiam mellis violasque rosasque:
    Qui venit hinc, prolis gaudia fructus habet.
Dicite apes teneræ, quàm dulce est ludere melle,
    Inter nectareos Dædala tecta fauos!
Quæ tamen hos lusus, quæ dulcia gaudia præbent,
    Matribus hæc tanti mella parasse fuit.
Vidi ego sic iuuenes curâ gaudere Magistri,
    Queis fuit alterius dulce labore frui.

The Jesuit Latin Poets gather Honey from the Classics

Giannantonio Bernardi
(1670-1743)

Giannantonio Bernardi was born at Padua on April 19, 1670. After entering the Society of Jesus at 17 years of age on January 3, 1687, he taught rhetoric in Venice, was a professor of philosophy for six years at Parma, and a professor of theology at Bologna for six years. He pronounced his final vows in the Society of Jesus on February 2, 1704. He accompanied Carlo Ruzzini, his penitent and eventual doge of Venice (1732-35) on an embassy to Constantinople in 1712-13. Bernardi's *Elegy* II.3 is a description of that city. Upon the death of Fr. Joseph Jouvancy in 1719, the Father General, Michael Tamburini, was on the point of summoning Bernardi to work as his personal secretary and composer of the *Historia Societatis (History of the Society),* but Bernardi's health would not allow this. Instead, Bernardi stayed in northern Italy and served as rector at Mantua, director of studies at Busseto, and superior of the professed house at Venice.

Most of Bernardi's literary productions are collected in his *Carmina (Poems),* published in 1715 at Bologna. There are two books of elegies, some of which are comparisons of classical authors, a favorite theme of Bernardi. There is one book of *Sermones (Conversations)* and one of *Odarum et epigrammatum (Odes and Epigrams).* Bernardi included a revision of his poem on *Prudentia (Prudence),* first published when he was teaching philosophy at Parma. Finally, the work contains comparisons, written in prose, of Cicero and Tacitus and Cicero and Seneca. These essays are in the form of inaugural addresses for the school year.

Giannantonio Bernardi had a career much like that of the other Jesuit Latin poets in our collection: he was a teacher, a preacher, and a confessor to the nobility. He passed away at Bologna on July 26, 1743.

Poem 58

Epigramma

Ad senem quemdam formae suae studiosissimum

    Quem te, vane senex, dicam; cui pluris habetur
        Iudicio capitis iudicium speculi?
    Iam pater est alter solitus te dicere patrem;
        Iamque nepos dudum te vocat alter avum.
5   Magna tamen (quis credat?) adhuc tibi cura placendi est.
        Vix Paris ad cultus ipse, quod addat, habet.
    Mitto leves phaleras, et vix florentibus annis
        Dignam, qua gaudes pulchrior ire, togam.
    Cura comae potior. Mos est tibi radere canos,
10 Ut maior sit frons inde, minusque caput.
    Quas Anglae misere nurus, Germanave virgo,
        Succedent flavae, silva parata, comae,
    Nec satis hoc: Cypri conspergitur imbre minutae
        Aurea caesaries, parsque propinqua togae.
15 Quin glabro prius aufertur seges hispida mento,
        Et vulsas pumex laevigat usque genas.
    Tyndaridum Paridumque hinc blandis coetibus adstas,
        Blandior ipse; frequens risus utrisque licet.
    Qui putet esse senem, vix est tamen ullus in illis;
20 Vix ullus, qui te nunc putet esse virum.
    Unde virum credant, cui tota femina vultu!
        Cui melior capitis pars, aliena coma est?

Meter: Elegiac distich

Title: Bernardi's epigrams, like so many of the ancients', are used as instruments of attack. The use of a wig is a common object of satire in the 17th and 18th centuries.

Poem 58

Epigram

The Old Man - A Fop

You vain old fool! What shall I say? You rely more on a mirror than on the common judgment of prudent men. Here is one father who calls you his own father and your grandson who calls you his grandfather. Who would believe it? And you are still interested in your own good looks. (5) Even Paris himself has reached the limit.

I am not speaking of your bright baubles, of a dress hardly suitable to your years, the London cut of your suit, the care you give your hair. You have a habit of tearing out the gray hairs to appear younger or to have a bigger forehead! (10) What English girl or German girl will supply you with blond hair for a hairdo? And this isn't all. This hairdo must be sprinkled with golden spangles on the collar.

First of all your dark face has to be razored (15) and your cheeks smoothed with pumice. And here you stand all polished, like one of the group of followers of Tyndareus and Paris. Both of them laugh at you. Everyone knows you are an old man. How can they believe you are a real man (20) with a face like a woman's? – whose better part of hair is someone else's.

Text:

2. Looks, appearance *(iudicium speculi)* are more important to this old man than common sense *(iudicio capitis)*.
3. In other words, the old man is a grandfather.
4. *iamque...dudum:* for a long time now; the old man is not a recent grandfather.
6. *Paris:* Paris or Alexander, Helen's seducer, is the "hero of beauty".
7. *phaleras:* medallions, medals.
9. *canos:* Understand *capillos:* gray hairs.
11. *nurus:* need not be "daughters-in-law"; "young women" will do (or possibly "granddaughters-in-law").
13. *Cypri...imbre:* with a shower of cyprus-ointment. The *Cyprus* or *Cyprinum* was a fragrant oil made from the blossoms of the cypress tree.
15. *seges hispida:* facial hair, beard.
16. *laevigat:* alternate spelling for *levigat,* he makes smooth.
17. *Tyndaridum:* Castor and Pollux. They seem to be guilty of foppishness by association with their sister Helen and her paramour Paris.
19-20. Far from thinking him old, one scarce considers the subject a man, so decked out is he.

The Stream Sebethus (Fiume della Maddalena) with Vesuvius in the Background

Giacomo Lubrani
(1619-1693)

Giacomo Lubrani was born at Naples in 1619. At a young age, he entered the Society of Jesus at Naples on April 30, 1635. Most of his apostolic work took place in Naples where he taught grammar and humanities, but excelled in preaching. Among his sermons are panegyrics of the Saints of the Society of Jesus, funeral orations for Philip IV, king of Spain and Sicily, and Lenten sermons. Lubrani's poetic works were gathered in *Suaviludia Musarum ad Sebethi ripam. Epigrammaton libri X* (Naples, 1690) *(Pleasant diversions of the Muses at the Bank of the Sebethus. Ten Books of Epigrams.)* (The Sebethus is a small stream, flowing into the Bay of Naples.) In the dedicatory letter to the collection, Lubrani remarks on the problem of obscenity in Martial and Catullus, the models for the Latin epigrammatist. With regard to form, he modeled himself on the former, especially, and wrote mostly two- to six-line poems. Book 10 of the collection consists entirely of two-line tags for gifts, called *Xenia (Guest Gifts)* in imitation of Martial's Book 13.

Although better known in his day as a preacher, Lubrani did write smooth, elegant Latin verse. He passed away in Naples on October 23, 1693.

Poem 59

Liber V, Epigramma LXIII
S. Philippus Nerius aulicos Romae revocat ab ambitu utens bissyllabo: Quid tum?

    Proiectoria regnat ars in aulis.
    Nam Fortuna dolo pecunioso
    Captat blanda pedes; opima verbis,
    Nunquam rem loquitur: per alta praeceps
5   Imis aequat arenulis colossos;
    Sacra hinc Nerius emphasi disertus
    Sermonum phaleras perosus omnes.
    Veri Suada, medulla gratiarum,
    Binis carmine syllabis, biformes
10 Delevit fatui strophas honoris.
    Romae vota facis cliens, mathesis
    An te fidere ducit auspicato?
    An census, et imagines avorum?
    An dos mentis, et eruditiones?
15 Sit factum bene: ad infulas via haec est.
    Quid tum? culmina summa Vaticani
    Ascendes, triplici potens tiara:
    Quid tum? Maxime, iure mortuali
    Debebis cinerem putrem sepulchro.
20 Aeque plebs Tiberina, praesulesque
    Marcent exigua pares in urna.

---

1. *Prophecy:* foretelling; 9-10 *cut through...sayings:* settled all double-meaning words; 20. *the poverty along the Tiber:* and all the Tiber world.

Meter: Hendecasyllabic or Phalaecean

Title: Mertz originally translated, "Philip Neri checks place-seekers". *Aulici*, courtiers, need not be pejorative, but they certainly are the butt of this piece.

Poem 59

Book 5, Epigram 63
Philip Neri moderates ambition with two syllables: What then?

The art of Prophecy ranks high in the halls of nobles. Fortune, beguiled by money, trips up the feet; she's very clever with words; she never states things as they are; she levels your grandees even with the smallest speck of dust. (5) Neri, well versed in sacred lore, was a champion of truth and hated all pretense of language. He cut through all ambiguous sayings with a refrain of two syllables: "What then?" (10)

You are a client in Rome and you make your play for position. Is it the stars or astrology that makes you so confident? Is it wealth, or do you rely on the pictured story of your ancestors? Or is it the gift of intellect and your educational equipment? Suppose it is.

This way will lead you to the trappings of priestly honors. (15) "What then?" You'll reach the highest dignity in the Vatican, even the triple tiara. "What then?" At the best you are subject to the law of death. Your ashes will go to the tomb; the poverty along the Tiber (20) and the excellence of the prelate's station will equally moulder away in a small urn.

Text:

1. *Proiectoria...ars:* The art of "throwing, casting down *(ambitions)*". The art of prophecy would have been *coniectoria ars.*

5. *arenulis:* for *harenulis,* grains of sand.

6. *emphasi:* rhetorical stress.

6. *Nerius:* St. Philip Neri (1515-1596) was a mainstay of the Counter-Reformation and he worked especially with the clergy of Rome, many of whom may have had the ambitions satirized in the poem.

7. *sermonum phaleras:* bombastic speech.

8. *Suada:* the goddess of Persuasion. Here it is used of Philip Neri with the force of "swayer of truth". Cicero, citing Ennius, speaks of *suadae medulla,* "the quintessence of eloquence". *(Brutus.* 58).

10. *strophas:* tricks, artifices.

11. *mathesis:* astrology.

12. *auspicato:* an adverb here: auspiciously, under good omen.

15. *infulas:* fillets; the word is used here for advancement in an ecclesiastical career.

Poem 60

Liber V, Epigramma LXXVII
De nivatis per aestatem potionibus

    Brumae delicias voluptuosae
    Augustis gula provocat Kalendis,
    Sub caelo glacies caniculari
    Per coenacula sumptuosiorum
5 Lautam fert hiemem, Alpiumque poenae
    Ningunt gaudia diviti popinae.
    Frigescunt patinae, calentque fauces.
    Convivae Rhodopen bibunt, eduntque
    Mixtam ad pocula rasilis Falerni.
10 Callosumque acuunt gelu palatum,
    Exorbentque sitim. Sagaxne tantum
    Ausa est ganea blandiente luxu,
    Ut nix urere posset helluones?

---

3. *of the rich:* of the richer classes; 12. *with blandishing extravagance:* with alluring ads; 11-12. *enterprising brothel:* wide-awake restaurateur; 12. *brothel:* eatery; 13. *to consume with passion the gluttons:* to set afire the heat of the gourmet.

Meter: Hendecasyllabic or Phalaecean

Title: Strictly, the wine is cooled with snow *(nivatis)*, not with ice.

Poem 60

Book 5, Epigram 77
Iced drinks in the summertime

On the first of August, your glutton calls for the delights of winter. In the dog days in the halls of the rich either ice supplies the satisfying tastes of winter or the glaciers of the Alps (5) supply the pleasures of a rich table.

The dishes are chilled; appetites are stimulated; guests drink Rosé wine and eat dainty hors d'oevres, and the dry palates are wetted down with the finest choice Falernian. (10)

Is it only the enterprising brothel that dares with blandishing extravagance to use ice to consume with passion the gluttons?

Text:

1. *voluptuosae:* The epithet is transferred from "delights" to "winter".
2. *Augustis...Kalendis:* August 1.
3. *caelo...caniculari:* the dog-star days, which occur in August.
4. *coenacula:* alternate for *cenacula,* the dining room of the rich *(sumptuosiorum).*
5. *lautam...hiemem:* luxurious winter; but the luxury more properly consists in drinking cooled drinks in the summertime.
5. *Alpium poenae:* fines or levies paid by the Alps.
6. *popina:* eatery; it is used metaphorically for the rich man's banquet hall.
7. *calentque fauces:* "the throats grow warm" through drinking.
8. *Rhodopen:* Mt. Rhodope, a Thracian mountain. Lubrani means the snow from the north that has kept until August. "They drink icewater from Rhodope."
9. *rasilis Falerni:* of smooth Falernian.
10. *callosum:* here, "jaded".
12. *ganea:* "eating house" with the bad reputation as an abode of prostitutes. Lubrani sarcastically calls the rich man's dining room a *ganea.*
13. *nix urere:* Lubrani dwells on the paradox that "snow fires" passion. This quality of snow is a commonplace in medieval and humanistic poetry.

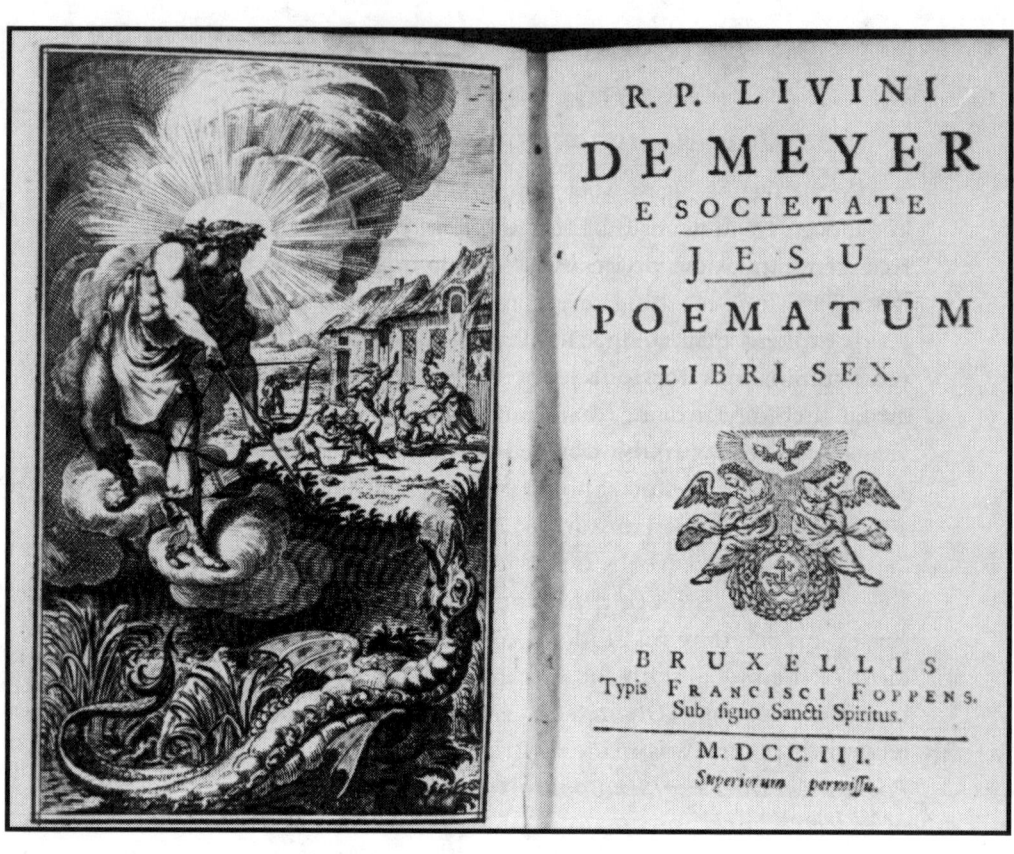

A Struggle of Spiritual Forces

Lieven De Meyere
(1655-1730)

Lieven De Meyere was born at Ghent on February 25, 1655. He entered the Society of Jesus at Mechlin on September 26, 1673. During his long teaching career, most of which was spent at the Jesuit College at Louvain, De Meyere taught humanities for six years, philosophy for four years, Sacred Scripture for one year, moral theology for one year, and scholastic theology for four years. For eight years he was dean and had two separate terms as rector at the Jesuit scholasticate at Louvain (1706-09 and 1710-14). He died at Louvain on March 19, 1730.

The published works of Lieven De Meyere are quite extensive. A major portion of these consists of a series of theological theses, prepared by his students for public defences at Louvain. Most of them deal with the sacrament of penance and the controversies on grace *(De auxiliis, On Helps)*. The first major collection of poetry was made at Brussels in 1703 under the title, *Poematum libri sex (Six Books of Poems)*. The first three books of this collection are a revision of De Meyere's work *De ira (On Anger)*. There are also two books of elegies and one of lyric verses. He informed the reader that he was working on still other poems, but they were not yet ready for publication. These appeared, undoubtedly, in the 1727 edition in 12 books. In the *De institutione principis libri III (On the Training of the Prince)*, De Meyere used dactylic hexameters.

With De Hossche and Vande Walle, De Meyere is considered one of the best neo-Latin poets of the Southern Netherlands. He modeled himself on Propertius and strove for classical perfection in form and diction. In controversy, De Meyere was the unrelenting opponent of those infected with Pelagianism and the steadfast foe of the Jansenists.

Poem 61

Liber I, Ode VI
Horatii Principis Lyricorum Laudes

Flacce, lyra cantuque potens haerentia vivis
   Movere saxa rupibus,
      Threiciumque nemus

Carmine nativis traducere montibus, ut qui
5   Acheronta rupit Orpheus;
      Thracia quem Rhodope

Olim admirata est animos mollire ferarum,
   Tu Pindaro potentior
      Carmen ad Ausonios

10 Deducis numeros varia testudine vates:
   Ut nuper ales Daulias
      Caedem Ityli memorans,

Omnia Daedaleo discrimina gutture vocum
   Princeps recenset alitum:
15   Sic lyra pulsa manu

Nil humile aut enerve sonat; sublimis et audax
   Vexare cantu sidera.
      Sive agitas vitium

Censor, et errantis mordes commissa iuventae,
20   Morum peritus arbiter:
      Aurea sive canis

Observanda sacris quondam praecepta poetis,
   Non posteris exactius
      Graecia liquit opus:

---

19. *keenly...misdeeds:* you break down the sins of youth.

Meter: Unusual tristich stanzas, consisting of 1.) a dactylic hexameter; 2.) an iambic dimeter; and 3.) a dactylic catalectic trimeter.

Title: It is fitting that our last poet sings in praise of Horace whom so many of the Jesuit Latin poets imitated. Mertz observed, "Only certain lines are translated", and the version is more a detailed summary than a translation.

Poem 60

Book 1, Ode 6
Praise of Horace, Prince of Poets

Flaccus, skilled in lyre and song
  To move rocks from the cliffs and groves of Thrace
    And transfer them from their native mountains, (5)

More powerful than Pindar
  You brought his music to Italy
    And poets with their various meters. (10)

There is nothing weak, nothing dull;
  With head erect and boldly
    You challenge the very stars. (17)

You challenge and condemn vice
  As a censor, and
    Keenly adjudicate the misdeeds of youth.

You sing of the golden precept left to the poets. (20)
  Greece was not more insistent in leaving
    Its work to its descendants.

Text:

3. *Threiciumque nemus:* the Thracian grove is the land of Orpheus, Horace's and the other lyric poets' predecessor in the genre.

5. *Acheronta rupit:* "burst (the bonds) of Acheron". De Meyere alludes to Orpheus' rescue of Eurydice from the underworld.

6. *Rhodope:* a mountain range in Thrace (today Despoto Dagh); part of the Haemus (today the Great Balkan range).

11. *ales Daulias:* "the Daulian bird" is Procne, who, in the Roman version of the myth, was changed into a swallow.

12. *Ityli:* As Catullus at 65.13 so De Meyere confuses Itylus, son of Zethus, with Itys, Procne's son.

25 Aut Maecenati si comis epistola fertur
        Legenda vel Neronibus;
            Omnia plena Deo,

    Gratiaque utilitasque comesque ambobus honestum;
        Decorque qui vulgum latet,
30   Sidereusque furor,

    Singula divini sunt ornamenta poetae,
        Cui Roma vix tulit parem,
            Saecula nulla ferent.

Text:

25. *Maecenati:* Maecenas was Horace's patron to whom he dedicated so much of his work. His name is synonymous with literary patron.

28. The serious, moral purpose of poetry that Horace advocated in his *Ars Poetica* is accepted wholeheartedly by the Jesuit Latin poets.

If a letter is to be delivered to Maecenas (25)
   Or someone in power,
     Everything has the touch of the deity:

Grace, helpful suggestion, charm, sincerity,
   Real excellence which escapes the common folk,
     Even a heavenly frenzy. (30)

All these points mark the poet divine.
   Rome scarcely gave an equal
     And no age in the future will.

Poem 62

Liber I, Ode VII
In Podagram
Eius dolores acutissimos ac incurabiles esse

      Quae dira pestis ossa corrodit mea?
         Quae missa Cocyto lues
      Acrem et tenaci glutine adstrictum intimis
         Nervis furorem dividit?
5   Expressa num quis viperis mordacibus
         Venena porrexit mihi?
      Potensve saga toxicum nocentius
         Nostro cruore miscuit?
      Non si caminis corpus Aetnaeis sonet,
10   Et monte Cyclopum premar,
      Bituminosis aut adurar ignibus
         Edace mixtis sulphure,
      Serpens medullis penitus exesis malum
         Inaestuet ferventius.
15   Noctem, et papaver vincit insomnis dolor:
         Nec molle pulvinar iuvat.
      Quin et tumorem siderum allapsus gravat,
         Et horridum silentium.
      Ferocientes interim morsus lues,
20   Iramque et arma duplicat.
      Dein mille velox, more Parthorum, vibrat
         (Heu fulminis vim!) spicula.
      Quod si minutis pallium contactibus
         Vel extimam radat cutem,

---

1. *terrible:* baneful; 18. *under the stars:* of the stars; 18. *as they decline:* in their decline; 21. *Parthians:* Medes.

Meter: Iambic strophe (alternating trimeters and dimeters).

Title: The Latin title suggests a hostile attack: "Against Gout, Painful and Incurable".

Poem 62

Book I, Ode 7
The Agony and Hopelessness of Gout

What is this terrible thing that is tearing my bones apart?
    What is this plague come from the river of woe?
It hits every nerve fiber with its steady ache.
    Has someone handed me poison with a viper's sting? (5)
Has some grand witch mixed a more harmful potion in my blood?
    If my body were in the forges of Aetna
Or pressed down by the mountains of the Cyclops (10)
    Or boiled in tar mixed with sulphur,
Nothing could cause more fever heat.
    A creeping pain is burning in my inmost being,
A steady pain destroys my rest at night;
    Not even poppy or a soft bed is any relief. (15)
The long weary hours under the stars as they decline
    Add their weight in the terrible silence of night.
Meanwhile the pestilential bite grows and increases
    And brings about a feeling of anger. (20)
The disease, like the Parthians of old, shoots a thousand arrows!
    Oh, the power of these flashes like lightning!
Even the blanket causes pain if it but touch the skin.

Text:

2. *Cocyto:* Cocytus, the river of lamentation in Hades.

3. *tenaci glutine:* with adhering glue; the gout is depicted as clinging to the victim's sinews and inner organs.

7. *saga:* fortune-teller, wise woman; here: witch.

9-10. *caminis...Aetnaeis...et monte Cyclopum:* the forge of Vulcan and the Cyclopes under Mt. Aetna. De Meyere refers to the sudden shafts of pain from the gout.

15-18. The still calm of the night does not relieve, but even heightens the suffering of the gout-victim.

19. *ferocientes:* from *ferocire,* to rage, to be furious. It is a pre-classical and post-classical word.

21-22. The gout, like the Parthian cavalrymen, attacks with a shower of arrows *(mille...spicula).*

25   Quis credat? et virilis eiulatio
        Clamore tormentum levat
     Nullumque tantis luctibus solatium
        Adfert amicorum cohors,
     Praeter iocos risusque languenti graves.
30   Nil et Machaon adiuvat,
     Fastidiosis inclytus liquoribus
        Lenire morbos ceteros.
     O! quis podagram mitis afflictis Deus
        Ad ima vertat Tartara!
35   Tormenta quid diversa vates fingitis?
        Cur Sisyphum vexat lapis,
     Fugaxque ramus Tantalum? Poena omnibus
        Haec una sit nocentibus.

Text:

30. *Machaon:* the famous surgeon of the Greeks at Troy.

33-38. The pain of the gout is so bad that De Meyere suggests it replace the torments of Sisyphus (*lapis,* stone) and Tantalus (*ramus,* the unattainable branch).

Who'll believe it? And all my manly cry does not ease the
    torment; (25)
No, nor do the visiting friends with their laughter and cheer;
    Not even Machaon, (30) famous for his soothing ointments for
        other pains.
Oh, that some kind god, good to the sick, would send gout to
    hell!
    Yes, you poets, why dream up other torments? (35)
Why does the stone worry Sisyphus, or the tree branch Tantalus?
    Gout is the one sole punishment for all.

---

31. *famous:* so well known.

INDEX OF *INCIPITS*

A

Adeste, magni carceris incolae	**35,**	p. 112
Ah sitio! clamas: absunt his rupibus undae	**18a,**	p. 48
Albis dormiit in rosis	**6,**	p. 16
Amemus. An Massylus, aut nostris riget	**16,**	p. 42
Anglia iudiciis scelerata, et caede nefanda	**19,**	p. 54

B

Bis tibi sum genetrix, nam bis tibi luminis auras	**22,**	p. 60
Brumae delicias voluptuosae	**60,**	p. 210

C

Cervice torta, mille carnifex modis	**27,**	p. 78
Cives Hymetti, gratus Atticae lepos	**10,**	p. 30
Corpus fatiscit, pondus inutile	**25,**	p. 70
Cum meam nullis humeros onustus	**11,**	p. 32

D

De nocte quidam subditus Amoris iugo	**51,**	p. 182
Dicebas abiens: Sponsa vale; simul	**13,**	p. 36
Dum per vireta Cypri	**49,**	p. 172

E

Eheu, Telephe, ludimur	**2,**	p. 6
En horret gelidus saevis Aquilonibus aether	**20,**	p. 56
En male, continuo numquam lassata recursu	**21,**	p. 58
Et fugis, et fugiens clamas: Quid, Sponsa, moraris?	**18d,**	p. 48

F

Flacce, lyra cantuque potens haerentia vivis	**61**	p. 214
Fons innocenti lucidus magis vitro	**15,**	p. 40

H

Hic iaceo, rigidae prostratus vulnere mortis	**57**	p. 200
Hic ille Morus, quo melius nihil	**31,**	p. 100
Humanae solers imitator, psittace, linguae!	**50,**	p. 176

I

Iamque adeo toti nutu pendemus ab uno	**41,**	p. 136
Imperium sine fine datum tibi Roma perenne est	**54,**	p. 190

L

Lugete, 0 Charites, Ioci, Lepores	**48,**	p. 170

M

Mansuete Mortis frater, eburneae	**38,**	p. 124
Me stipate rosariis	**7,**	p. 20
Meo beatus, cetera vilibus	**5,**	p. 14
Mollis vellere serici	**46,**	p. 160
Multun Quinctus emit, sed caecum, Cosmice mulum	**18e,**	p. 50

N

Non me Democriti sales	**8,**	p. 24
Non nuda vox amicus est, non cassa nux	**24,**	p. 66
Non potest iussus tria dicere verba Philippus	**18f,**	p. 50

O

O Diva, vitae praeses et altera	**42,**	p. 140
O gratos mihi, gratiisque plenos	**30,**	p. 94
O nata Capri sidere frigido	**33,**	p. 106
O quae, populea summa sedens coma	**14,**	p. 38
O quae virenti graminis in toro	**44,**	p. 150

P

Placidi rores matutini	**17,**	p. 44
Proiectoria regnat ars in aulis	**59,**	p. 208
Puelle, seu te progenuit novus	**36,**	p. 116
Pulsabat digitis lyram lyristes	**56,**	p. 198

Q

Quae dira pestis ossa corrodit mea?	**62,**	p. 218
Quae tegit canas modo bruma valles	**3,**	p. 10
Quem te, vane senex, dicam; cui pluris habetur	**58,**	p. 204

Quid nocti lumen, luci quid quaerimus umbram?	**18c,**	p. 48
Quid? si beatis Mentibus asseri	**43,**	p. 144
Quid Stagyra iuverit	**26,**	p. 72
Quis credat? stygio proximus ostio	**45,**	p. 156
Quis novum hic caelo suspendit Daedalus alas?	**55,**	p. 194
Quo die terris properans relictis	**39,**	p. 130
Quod et procellas inter et aspera	**47,**	p. 166
Quod nec psittacus audeat	**40,**	p. 132

R

RIdere amici vultis? ecce fabellam	**28,**	p. 82

S

Saltemus, socias iungite dexteras	**37,**	p. 120
Sic, Torquate, iaces merito sine honore sepulchri?	**52,**	p. 186
Siderum sacros imitata vultus	**12,**	p. 34
Sive te molli vehet aura vento	**9,**	p. 28
Somne, quies animi, curarum, Somne iuvamen	**29,**	p. 88
Sonora buxi filia sutilis	**4,**	p. 12
Soror Galeni, vivida sanitas	**34,**	p. 108

U

Unde pax mihi tanta, Laure, quaeris	**23,**	p. 64
Ut scires, quo, Christe, tui flammarer amore	**18b,**	p. 48

V

Videmus Oenotrias arces, eversa duello	**53,**	p. 188
Vinum Falerno nectare dulcius	**32,**	p. 104
Vive iucundae metuens iuventae	**1,**	p. 4

INDEX OF NAMES AND THEMES

A

Abad, Diego, ix
Aesop, 181
Albert of Bavaria, 116
Anacreon, 172
Apuleius, 79
Aristotle, 73, 149, 185
Ars Poetica, viii, 95, 216
Augustine, St., 60-61
Avancini, Nicolas, xv, 68-75

B

Balde, Jacob, vii, ix, xv, 53, 96-147
Bandusia, 41
Barberini, Francesco, 3
Barberini, Maffeo, 2, 30
Bauhusius: see Van Bauhuysen
beer, 106, 107
bees, 2, 30, 31
Berchmans, John, 85
Bernardi, Giannantonio, 202-205
Bettini, Mario, 44
Bidermann, Jacob, 63
Blandusia, 41
Blessed Virgin, viii, 3, 22, 34, 35, 36, 42, 43, 70, 71, 86, 87, 98, 130, 131, 140-143
Boleyn, Anne, 101
Bona Mors Society, 140
Braceland, Lawrence, 39
breviary hymns, 2, 41, 185
brevity of life, ix, 10
Brower, Christopher, 154
Browne, Valerie, ix

C

Cabilliau, B., 63
Campion, Edmund, ix
canary, 171
Caraffa, V. 140
Catullus, 41, 170, 171, 207, 215
Charles I, 54, 55
Chilo, 74
cicada, ix, 3, 38, 39, 150, 151, 198, 199
Cicero, 29, 35, 138, 149, 203, 209
Clarke, John, 83
Claudian, 98
Corneille, Pierre, 165
Coster, F., xv, 78, 79
Cromwell, Oliver, 54

D

Dauphin, 165
De Hossche, S. xv, 53, 84-91, 92, 93, 95, 213
De Meyere, Lieven, xvi, 212-221
Democritus, 25
Demosthenes, 149
Desbillons, F.J.T., xv, 180-183
De Wael, W., 85-87
doctor, 58, 59

E

England, 54, 55
Ennius, 17, 209

F

Festle, John, 78
fever, 58, 59
finch, 132-135
fortitude, ix
fortune, ix, 6-9, 28, 29
friendship, 64, 65

G

Galen, 109

Galluzzi, Tarquinio, xv, 2, 184-191
Gonzaga, Aloysius, 48
gout, 218-221
Grace, Michael, ix, x
greed, 160-63
Guiniggi, Vincenzo, xv, 192-201

H

Hamy, Alfred, xv
happy death, 140-143
haughtiness, 160-163
heliotrope, 136-139
Heraclitus, 25
Herder, 98
Herodotus, 165
Homer, 134
Horace, vi, viii, 2, 3, 5, 7, 13, 30, 35, 37, 40, 43, 69, 93, 95, 98, 100, 106, 107, 141, 168, 195, 214-217

I

iced drinks, 210, 211
IJsewijn, Jozef, viii, 83
Imago primi saeculi, ix, xv, xvi

J

Jansenists, 149, 213
Jesuit theater, 69, 98, 99, 154, 164, 193
Jesuitica, vii, xv
Jouvancy, Joseph, 203
Justinus, 165
Juvenal, 5, 25, 113, 114

K

Kane, William T., vii
Karl Theodor, 181
Kreihing, J., 52-61
Krug, Kathryn, viii

L

Ladislaus IV, 2 3, 77
La Fontaine, 181
Landivar, Rafael, ix

Lauder, William, 153
Leopold I, 53
Leopold William, 86
Lessius, Leonard, 86
Lewinski, S., 4, 32
life, brevity of, ix, 10
Livy, 126, 149
Louis XIII, 77
Louis XIV, 165-167, 169
Louis XV, 169
Lubienski, S., 3
Lubrani, Giacomo, xvi, 206-211
Lucan, 141
lyre, ix, 12, 13, 198, 199

M

Madonna della Strada, vi, vii
Majeske, Donna, viii
Malapert, Charles, 63, 76-83
Marc'hadour, G., 100
Martial, 48, 53, 207
Masen, Jacob, xv, 152-163
Middleton, Alice, 101
Milton, John, 153
Monica, St., 60, 61
More, Thomas St., 100-103

N

nature, praise of, ix
Narew, 16
Neri, Philip St., 208-209
Noyelle, Charles de, 69

O

Orlandini, Nicholas, 193
Osiander, Lucas, 78-79
Ovid, 53, 89, 106, 137

P

Panaetius, 25
parrot, 176-179
peace of soul, 64, 65
Petrucci, Girolamo, 2
Phaedrus, 181
Philip IV, 77, 207
Philip Wilhelm, 98
Pindar, 3, 53
Plato, 149

Plautus, 71, 98, 154
Pliny the Elder, 57
Polygnotus, 73
Porée, P. de la, 168
Praxiteles, 117
pride, 160-163
Propertius, 53, 213
Prudentius, vii
Puy, Henri du, 63
Pythagoras, 25

Q

Quintilian, 98

R

Ramus, Daniel, 174-179
Rapin, René, xv, 148-151
Reiffenberg, F. , xv, 175
Rooney, Clare, 124, 130
rope dancer, 194-197
Roper, Margaret, 101
Roper, William, 101
rose, 3, 34, 35
Rue, Charles de la, xv, 164-167
Ruzzini, Carlo, 203

S

Sacchini, F., 193
salamander, 57
Sanadon, Nicholas, 168
Sanadon, Noel Étienne, 168-173
Sarbiewski, C., vii, ix, 1-51, 53, 87, 93, 97, 98
Schor, Patti, xv
seasons, ix, 11, 56, 57
self-knowledge, 72, 73
Seneca, 203
Shakespeare, 7, 12, 14, 64, 73, 156
sickness, 70, 71
Silviludium (pl.: -a), 3, 44, 144, 145
sleep, 88-91, 124-129
Socrates, 73
Solon, 74
Song of Songs, 20-23, 36, 37, 48, 49, 130, 131

Southwell, Robert, ix
Sparrow, John, 44
Statius, 98, 117, 133, 176, 177
Strada, Famiano, 2
sufficiency of virtue, ix

T

Tacitus, 203
Tamburini, Michael, 203
Tasso, Torquato, 186-187
Theocritus, 148
thinness, 108, 109
Thucydides, 149
Tibullus, 53
tightrope walker,. 194-197

U

Urban VIII, 2, 3, 20, 30, 185

V

Van Bauhuysen, Bernard, xv, 62-67, 74
Van der Beke, W., 53
Vande Walle, Jacob, 20, 86, 93-95, 176, 213
Varro, 79
violet, 3
Virgil, 5, 55, 67, 105, 114, 117, 165, 167, 171, 185, 191
Vitelleschi, Mucius, 193

W

Wall, 4
wine, 104, 105
winter, 56, 57

Z

Zaccharia, 175
Zeno, 73

DATE DUE			
9-19-06			
11/26/06			